CW01020393

Curious

CROUCH END

Curious Crouch End
Andrew Whitehead

Copyright © Andrew Whitehead 2021

Published in 2021 by
Five Leaves Publications,
14a Long Row, Nottingham NG1 2DH
www.fiveleaves.co.uk
www.fiveleavesbookshop.co.uk

ISBN: 978-1-910170-83-0

Printed in Great Britain

Curious

CROUCH END

Andrew Whitehead

Five Leaves Publications

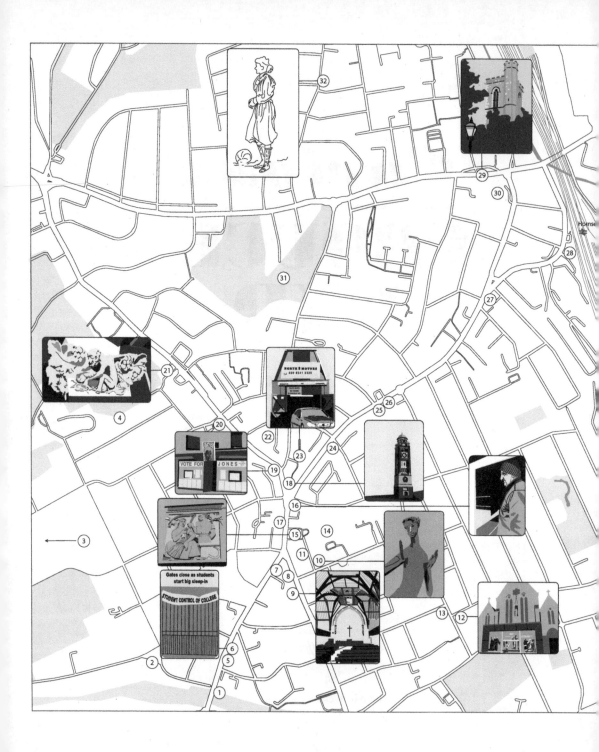

CONTENTS

Introduction

"I'm sorry to trigger collective heart failure in Crouch End," wrote Sali Hughes in the *Observer*, "but sourdough is overrated." Whether she's right about baking or indeed the wellbeing of Crouch Enders, she certainly reflects how the world sees the place. It's leafy, liberal North London. It has a Waitrose, a fishmonger, several butchers and bakers, two cinemas almost side-by-side, and more bookshops, vinyl stores, florists and independent coffee shops per head of population than... well, you get the picture.

The trouble is that most people who live more than a mile or two off the W7 bus route don't know Crouch End too well. "Where on earth is it?" half of London asks. It's not on the tube map; there's never been a borough of Crouch End; or a Parliamentary constituency that has taken its name; there's no Crouch End College; and the biggest local school, Highgate Wood, pretends it's somewhere else.

Crouch End – with its echoes of anonymous Ponders End or Gerald Kersh's dystopian Fowlers End – conjures up an image of a remote outpost of London. The geography adds to this sense of isolation. Crouch End is surrounded on three sides by high ground. It's overlooked by the Northern Heights of London, but isn't quite up there with Highgate and Muswell Hill. The residents of Crouch End sometimes bask in this aloofness. It breeds a proud and intense localism – at least that's what I told my publisher when he asked me why anyone would be curious about Crouch End.

This has been amplified by what Crouch End has lost. It was once at the heart of one of the big outer London boroughs. It's home to perhaps the most ambitious of London's twentieth century town halls. And then within a generation, it was all snatched away. When in the 1960s Hornsey became part of the unwieldy new borough of Haringey – stretching awkwardly from Highgate to Tottenham Hale – so the municipal centre of gravity moved east. The Town Hall was reduced to hosting Saturday night hops. Crouch End was hollowed out.

In part, that's been a blessing. Benign neglect has its benefits. The area has escaped the worst ravages of urban redevelopment. It's a lively, friendly place, with lots of local shops and businesses. Many have been lost of course – among the most grievous being Paul Saxton's news stall, which closed while this book was being written – but the locality stands out for what it still has rather than what it once had. The churches are still standing, the pubs still serving and the admirable Hornsey Historical Society – much more than a Crouch End institution, though its heart and HQ lie here – encourages a pride in the urban heritage.

This is not a history of Crouch End. It's an exploration of what is curious about the area, and the stories which its buildings and streets reveal, or sometimes conceal. No attempt has been made to be comprehensive, so to those who believe that Christ Church, or Dunn's bakery, or the Lido, or the war memorial deserve attention, all I can say is: I absolutely agree. But not here.

There's the tricky question: where does Crouch End end? It melds imperceptibly into Hornsey, which is my excuse for including a couple of landmarks in Hornsey village even though some Hornsey-ites may wish to hold my feet to the flames. Some liberties have been taken. But having chanced across stories as remarkable as those of the footballer Nettie Honeyball and the rates defaulter Bridget Hitler, I wasn't going to fail to include them because of parochial impropriety.

My first instinct was to include even the Old Dairy, with its seven magnificent dairy-themed sgraffito panels. It is after all at an address on Crouch Hill. But a distinguished Crouch Ender declared that well out of bounds: "different borough, different postcode, different place altogether!"

Crouch Enders and those interested in the area and its history will be familiar with some of the places and episodes recounted here – but I'd be disappointed if even the most devoted Crouch Ender fails to find much that's new and arresting. It's both a celebration of the area and an invitation to walk the streets more attentively, more curiously: you never know what you will come across.

Andrew Whitehead

1 | The Ghost Station

New York has the High Line – that stylish walkway along almost one-and-a-half miles of what was until the 1980s an elevated freight line. Well, that's nothing! North London has the Parkland Walk, another hugely imaginative repurposing of a disused rail line. And it's older, longer and altogether more luscious than its Transatlantic cousin.

The Walk, a nature reserve, stretches in two sections for a total of a little over four miles. The southern segment runs from twin tunnels (now a bat refuge) just south of Highgate Station to Finsbury Park. The broad walk- and cycle-way is so overshadowed by trees and shrubs that it feels wonderfully secluded – then just occasionally the walk bursts forth into the light offering a tantalising peep south to the City skyscrapers.

Halfway along this stretch is the highlight: a ghost station, both platforms still in place – but with no trains, no tracks and no ticket office. This is – or was – Crouch End Station, which sprang into life more than 150 years ago and passed into the afterlife of 'lost' stations a century or so later. It's now simply a forlorn relic of a lost era – the golden age when

Crouch End commuters could travel easily by train into town!

The Great Northern Railway opened Crouch End Station in August 1867 – providing an impetus for the building of smart villas in the area adjoining. It was on a short stretch of line from Finsbury Park to Highgate and, a little later, on to Alexandra Palace. Crouch Hill Station nearby is of similar vintage but on a different line – it's still open as a stopping point for the service along the vital artery linking Gospel Oak and Barking.

The line never quite achieved its potential in terms of passenger numbers, and in the mid-1930s a plan was devised to incorporate the track and stations into London Underground's Northern Line. Work on electrification was started but then halted early in the Second World War and subsequently abandoned. A peak-hours-only service was maintained using locomotives and rolling stock almost as old as the stations – but that simply staved off the inevitable, and Crouch End and the handful of other stations on the line closed to passenger traffic in July 1954.

The line south from Highgate was used for freight traffic for a few more years and then for the occasional transfer of tube carriages. The

last train of any sort to traverse through Crouch End Station was in September 1970, and within eighteen months all the track had been removed. The station's mainly timber-built platform shelter had already gone; the street-level ticket office, directly over the tracks on the crest of Crouch End Hill, was demolished in 1977. But you can still gain entrance here to the Parkland Walk and the rebuilt bridge, with a curious upside-down arch design, offers a commanding view over the disused platforms. The only other remnant which survives, with bricked-up windows, is what appears to have been the gents' toilets.

The Parkland Walk was officially opened in 1984 – fully a quarter-of-a-century before Manhattan's High Line – and has proved popular with cyclists, joggers and walkers (a section of it is part of the Capital Ring Walk) as well as with families out for a weekend stroll. And just to the east of the old station, there's a startling piece of public art: a Spriggan, no less, preparing to leap out from the recesses of the railway arches.

The Spriggan is a figure from Cornish folklore – and this one clearly missed the last train home.

2 | 1 Avenue Road

At first glance, they look like the ruins of a medieval monastery – not what you expect in Crouch End. On more leisurely inspection, you realise that these are remnants of one of the gothic-style villas which are still visible in this elevated part of the area (we are talking socially as well as geographically). The new building at 1 Avenue Road is sheltered housing, but part of the façade of the earlier incarnation of this address stands almost like a defensive barricade, the curtain wall of a castle perhaps, and the steps up to the original villa have been incorporated into the new design. It certainly adds interest to the streetscape.

This villa was built in the mid-1870s and consisted of a gargantuan fourteen rooms. Along with its contemporaries – several of which survive – it has those almost ecclesiastical architectural features which are the

11

hallmarks of mid-Victorian mock gothic: the sharp angles, the narrow Norman-style windows and the distinctly menacing silhouette.

There was something else a little menacing about the original 1 Avenue Road, which links it to the occult and the supernatural. In 1969, the building was badly damaged by fire. It was left unoccupied but the staircase was sufficiently intact to allow access to the upper floors. And of course, youngsters – and others – took advantage of that. The *Hornsey Journal*, with an eye on a winning headline, dubbed the derelict building 'the House of Dracula' and reported that "neighbours speak of strange goings-on at night and mysterious noises and flickering lights in upper windows."

The neighbours were right. There were strange goings-on. Della Farrant, a researcher into the paranormal who runs the 'Hidden

Highgate' website*, has the definitive account of just what was happening in a top floor room in the burnt-out villa. A small group of followers of the occultist Aleister Crowley held rituals and ceremonies there. The walls and floor were decorated in Crowleyesque fashion. Some care had been taken in the design and execution of these images, which included a heptagram in a circle, an eye in a pyramid, and various inscriptions and numbers including the inevitable 666.

We say definitive because Della's late husband David Farrant was one of the occultists involved in the rituals back in 1973. Three attempts were made to invoke the Greek god Pan – the final attempt being regarded as partially successful. These involved a certain amount of nudity – and yes, there is photographic evidence of that. David apparently didn't want to undertake the ritual in his own ceremonial space at home because the outcome was unpredictable. "I can understand why an uninhabited dwelling would be safer," says Della, who wasn't herself involved in the events. "I wouldn't want a sex-crazed Greek god marauding around my flat!" Indeed.

There were other reasons – Della Farrant believes – why 1 Avenue Road was chosen as the location. "Not only did the house look like a typical haunted house, it was genuinely haunted and would have had psychic energy to draw upon. It was also detached, and considering how LOUD the hymn to Pan is in parts, that would have been handy!"

It certainly spooked the neighbours. "A friend and I went into the house after it had been damaged," one woman commented. "We walked upstairs and saw the circle in the floor, realised it was not good and ran straight out!"

Tales still circulate that when developers tried to demolish the façade and the porch, there would be an accident or the machinery would stop working, and that's why those elements were incorporated into the new design. That may be a little far-fetched. But it does seem to have been some unnerving experiences of builders trying to stabilise the structure after the fire that gave the place the 'haunted' tag.

* https://hidden-highgate.org/

The bulk of the original building seems to have come down in the late 1970s, and local residents were involved in selecting the winning design for the new building. It's perhaps the conservation of at least some of the original gothic style which held sway. We're glad it did.

3 | Mrs Hitler

For decades now, parts of Crouch End have been described by estate agents as Highgate borders. Well, it's payback time. For our purposes, a sliver of Highgate is being redesignated Crouch End borders – just so that one of the craziest stories of this part of the world doesn't escape us.

In January 1939, hundreds of local residents appeared at court in Highgate after being summonsed by Hornsey Borough Council for non-payment of rates. Among them was a well-built woman in her late forties who ran a boarding house on Priory Gardens, just off Shepherds Hill. She had arrears of a little over £9. Her name was Mrs Bridget Hitler.

Bridget's brother-in-law was... yes, that Hitler. The man whose ideas of racial superiority and national destiny were about to plunge Europe, and much of the rest of the world, into war.

Bridget Dowling – at various times she also went by the names Brigid and Cissie – was born in Dublin and as a teenager came across an Austrian man working as a hotel porter. This was Alois Hitler, seven years older than his notorious step-brother, who had walked out of his home in Vienna at the age of fourteen after a row with his father and drifted into a life of petty crime.

In 1910, Bridget and Alois eloped to London where they married, and then moved to Liverpool, where their only child, William Patrick Hitler, was born. A few years later, Alois moved to Germany – alone. In the 1920s, having faked his own death and then married again, Alois Hitler was prosecuted for bigamy. It's said to have been Bridget's intervention that saved him from a jail sentence. When a young adult, Willy appears to have visited his uncle, though Adolf didn't make much effort to keep up with his family.

Bridget was left with no financial support from her husband, which is why – when living off Shepherds Hill – she took in lodgers. It seems to have been her main source of income. She appears to have managed to prise some money out of her brother-in-law: according to the historian Hugh Trevor-Roper (yes, the Hitler expert who made an ass of himself by authenticating the totally concocted 'Hitler Diaries') she got a modest allowance paid through the German Embassy and her son was given a fairly menial job with a German firm.

Perhaps that explains why, even when Adolf Hitler's name became reviled, Bridget was still happy to be known as Mrs Hitler and why she apparently had signed photos of Hitler in her home. Both Brigid Hitler and William Patrick Hitler are – somewhat incongruously – listed in the 1938 electoral register from 26 Priory Gardens, amid the good burghers of Highgate East.

Mrs Hitler's court appearance predictably prompted a flurry of newspaper interest. She was photographed in her kitchen cheerfully boiling a kettle against a backdrop of drying washing. "Nowadays it's a bit embarrassing being Mrs Hitler," she told the *Daily Express*. "Mind you, I've nothing to say against the Nazis as I've found them."

Two months after her court appearance, Bridget Hitler sailed to New York where she joined her son in a lecture tour designed to cash in on the family surname – and dismissed by the German authorities as a telling of "unauthenticated and detrimental tales of the Fuhrer." From then on the United States was her home. During the war, she rallied to the Allied cause and was photographed working in New York as a volunteer for the British War Relief Society. When Willy (also known as Patrick) enlisted, mother and son posed together, with the new recruit holding a newspaper bearing the banner headline: "TO HELL WITH HITLER".

Bridget may have made one more attempt to make money out of her surname. She (perhaps) wrote a book entitled *My Brother-in-Law Adolf*, which recounted how Adolf Hitler, when evading conscription in Austria, spent six months in Liverpool in 1911; how she introduced him to astrology; and how she persuaded him to trim the edges of his moustache and so was responsible for the toothbrush-style of upper lip which is forever associated with the Nazi leader.

The work was only published a decade after Bridget's death as *The Memoirs of Bridget Hitler*. Trevor-Roper dismissed it out-of-hand. The story of Adolf Hitler's sojourn in Liverpool was "unconvincing", he declared, though as this was a missing period in Hitler's life it could not be entirely disproven. And he was fairly certain that the memoirs weren't written by Bridget Hitler at all (though of course his record in identifying Hitler-related fakes is a long way from foolproof).

After the war, Bridget didn't want to be further tarnished by the Hitler name. She and her son took the name Stuart-Houston. She died in 1969 and is buried in Long Island; her son rests in the same grave.

4 | Shepherds Cot

Crouch End is surrounded on three sides by high ground – and where you get steepish slopes you often find rivers or streams. Indeed Hornsey Vale, which most Crouch Enders would see as part and parcel of their homeland, is a place name which almost demands running water. But there isn't any in N8 – not that you can see.

There was once. The Moselle – not to be confused with its much more substantial namesake in France – ran from west to east, from the 'northern heights' of Highgate and Muswell Hill (which gave its name to the stream) for seven miles or so until it entered the river Lea just beyond Tottenham Hale.

The Moselle has been christened Haringey's river – it's about the only thing that unites the borough's very different neighbourhoods. A pity, then, that it's one of London's lost rivers. It hasn't entirely disappeared, but there's very little on view. It has several tributary brooks, the most substantial in Queen's Wood – but after leaving these wooded glades, the Moselle doesn't again break surface until it appears, briefly, in the Lordship Rec. next to Tottenham's Broadwater Farm Estate.

These days, the various tributaries make their way underground – in culverts and in drains – meeting up at the Middle Lane end of Priory Park, then heading north – so, confusingly, away from Hornsey Vale –

and turning east, carried under the New River (which of course isn't a river at all but an artificial waterway intended to supply the growing city with drinking water) to Wood Green and on.

So Crouch End neither has the vineyards nor the vistas of that other Moselle valley. But it does have something rather precious – a large area of open space, about forty-five acres, between Wood Vale and Park Road either side of where London's Moselle once ran. This was once a farm, Shepherds Cot. A Hornsey borough publication of 1951 suggested that "some older residents may remember the last shepherd" tending his flock here.

Thanks to the foresight of municipal leaders in the 1890s, helped on by the bursting of a property bubble, most of this farmland escaped development and survives as park, playing fields, woodland and allotments, cared for and safeguarded very largely by volunteers. For an area of such space and charm, it really is hidden away – only one small section, Shepherds Hill Gardens, fronts on to a road of any consequence. This small park is a mix of sloping woodlands and a grassy area with striking views across the 'valley' to Alexandra Palace. It also displays in its topography just a trace of the ridge-and-furrow crop cultivation practised here many centuries ago.

Downhill from the gardens, on the most steeply sloping land, is the twenty-first century urban equivalent of ridge-and-furrow – Shepherds Hill Allotments, more than two-hundred of them, a thriving horticultural community which is home to bees and chickens too. It's not only hidden away, it hides away – a pity!

Beyond that is another patch of land owned by the London Borough of Haringey, the imaginatively named Crouch End Open Space, or CREOS, a pleasing mix of woodland and meadow. "A strange place which has slipped down the gap between one thing and another" – not our words, but those of Glenys Law, the chair of CREOS and, along with her fellow trustees of the charity, a volunteer.

The organisation once was the Crouch End Playing Fields Protection Society, and has over the decades metamorphosed in purpose from

protest to conservation. It's set up a woodland walk, put up signage and keeps this sliver of land as a common asset.

Part of this open space was once suburban tennis courts which have fallen to the depredations of silver birch and returned to their original wooded state. Most comes under Haringey's education department, and is – nominally, at least – for school use. But since the wood-fringed playing field here is so often a mud bath – not surprising given that one of the Moselle's lesser tributaries once made its way along the southern flank – it suits all parties for CREOS to care for the place.

The bulk of what was Shepherds Cot, the flat land closer to the centre of Crouch End, has been given over to playing fields for at least 130 years. Once church-owned land, it now provides grounds for five cricket clubs as well as three tennis clubs – a sporting oasis amid the urban sprawl. Here again there's a mosaic of different landholdings. Some of the clubs have commercial leases. The larger part is under the ownership and management of the Shepherds Cot Trust, set up in 1981 with a name that deliberately harks back to an earlier era.

"Our aim is to ensure that the place remains special – and that it doesn't get built on," says John Newton, the chair of the all-volunteer trustees representing the main sports clubs that play on the Trust's land. So far, they are succeeding on both counts. The area comes under the scope of Fields in Trust, better known by its old name of the National Playing Fields Association, which affords an extra layer of protection.

The former farmland has already suffered what some might describe as encroachment when what is now Highgate Wood School was built in the late 1950s and then extended in the '80s. More recently, a proposal to house several tennis courts under an inflatable – which would have been, in the words of one disapproving local resident, "about the size of an aircraft hangar" – has been seen off. A plan for floodlit five-a-side football pitches seems to have gone away, at least for the moment.

The Shepherds Cot Trust seeks to balance developing sports facilities against safeguarding what John Newton – who first got to know the area as a keen tennis player – describes as "a cherished site." If a cricketer suggests that the outfield isn't quite as smooth as it could be, they may well be reminded that the pitch was farmland not all that long ago.

And if anyone should wonder why the ground sometimes gets a little waterlogged, well, the Moselle river used to run just where second slip is now standing.

5 | '68 in N8

May '68. Revolution was in the air. Riots in Paris brought the French establishment to its knees and prompted a wave of student revolt across much of Europe. "We Shall Fight, We Will Win, Paris London Rome Berlin" – the dramatic front page of a newly established paper, *Black Dwarf*, caught the mood of the moment.

London's Sorbonne was an art school in N8. "On 10 May the French took over the Latin Quarter and, a few days later, the English took over the student canteen at Crouch End Hill," commented *Oz*'s Richard Neville with all the condescension he could muster. The 'Hornsey Revolution', as

some called it, was much more than that – it was a moment when students began to feel that the world was theirs to mould and transform.

"At first sight the college seems an unlikely setting for a revolution," *The Times* commented. "It is in a leafy suburb, full of trees and Victorian houses." For six weeks, students occupied and took control of Hornsey College of Art, without any violence and embracing a kind of direct democracy. And they had the enthusiastic support of several of their teachers.

"It was all incredibly exciting," recalls Jane Perryman, then a Hornsey student specialising in ceramics. "We got a frisson of a sense of power – it was the excitement of having some power."

Some of the key activists were keenly aware of what was happening in Paris. The Radical Students' Alliance was active at the college and there had been collections for the Vietnam Solidarity Campaign. A handful of students had joined the International Socialists, the precursor of the Socialist Workers Party. Tariq Ali, one of the founders of *Black Dwarf*, lived nearby and popped in from time-to-time. A week-long sit-in at the LSE had been the first expression of student protest on this side of the Channel – but that was simply the starter, while Hornsey College of Art was more like the main course.

Hornsey was hardly a copycat protest. Students on the far left were key figures in the sit-in, but most of those involved didn't see their action as an outright challenge to the established order. "Hornsey was a very sheltered place, as most art colleges were," says Martin Walker, then vice-president of the students' union who later came to consider himself an anarchist. "We never really talked about politics."

As is so often the case, the revolution in N8 was triggered above all by local grievances. But as is less often the case, the rugby club was in the vanguard. Hornsey was unusual for an art college in having a successful rugby team – and its captain, Kim Howells, was a left-wing activist (and later a Labour MP and minister). He persuaded the students' union to pay from its funds for new kit for the team, but the college bursar wouldn't authorise the payment.

The row over students' union autonomy extended to the college's refusal to grant a sabbatical year for the elected president, a Communist, Nick Wright. Also in the mix was unhappiness about plans to merge the college and a more widespread grievance about the ambiguous position of art education. Art colleges awarded degrees but didn't have the same status as universities; much of the teaching was focussed on the needs of industry rather than art and design; and money was short and facilities poor.

Hornsey College of Art had expanded rapidly – perhaps too rapidly. The imposing main building and site of the sit-in was on Crouch End Hill (the almost-semi-classical frontage dates from the 1930s, and the building was expanded in the '80s when it became the TUC's National Education Centre – it's now part of Coleridge Primary School). But most students were based in a string of half-a-dozen old, cold and cramped buildings – among them a disused air raid shelter – spread across North London. "The only time I was able to have contact with the hub of the college," says a graphics student from that time, "was when the so-called revolution took place."

"It felt very rigid," recalls Jane Perryman. "I had the perception that at art college you were exploring ideas and able to go into different mediums. But if you were doing three-dimensional design and wanted to use some photography, or something from the sculpture department, you couldn't. You weren't allowed. You felt very strait-jacketed. That was one of the reasons why the sit-in happened."

Not that it was planned. A student protest meeting was called at the main building on Crouch End Hill on 28th May to decide on a day of action or perhaps a teach-in. The college principal was OK with that. The gathering was so well attended, and so fervent, that those present decided on an immediate occupation.

"Five hundred students locked the gates, commandeered the North London college's telephone switchboard, took over the canteens and kitchens, [and] laid in a three-day stock of food," harrumphed the *Daily Express*.

23

"It was suggested that we sit-in but just until midday the next day, as nothing would be worse than it petering out," says David Poston, now a jewellery designer. "Discos and films were organised, as we planned to try and keep feckless art students on board. And for respectability there was a seminar on art education. That debate went on overnight and they reported back to the ad hoc general meeting and people were getting really angry." And the sit-in simply kept going.

The students' union was largely sidelined. A Students' Action Committee was set-up and decisions made at open daily meetings in the main hall. On the first full day of the sit-in, Martin Walker bowed out mid-afternoon: "What I remember most about the occupation is Manchester United playing Benfica." Walker, a Mancunian, had spent £9, a fortune for a student in the Sixties, on a ticket for the European Cup Final. He had never been to Wembley; he wasn't going to miss it. He arrived back at the college late in the evening pumped-up by United's victory in extra time – both George Best and Bobby Charlton scored – and went straight on the rostrum, seeking to inject urgency into a protest which was unsure of its purpose and direction.

The Hornsey revolution wasn't televised – but it was organised. A group of women students persuaded a store in Crouch End to provide groceries on sale or return. Within days, the bill had been paid off and the sit-in canteen was generating a modest profit. The phone switchboard was kept going. Other students organised music, speakers, discussions and screenings – the idea was to keep the college operating under student control.

Over the course of the occupation, public figures of the eminence of Nikolaus Pevsner and Buckminster Fuller addressed students. R.D. Laing, once described as "the counter-culture's favourite psychiatrist", turned up but declined to speak: "I've come to listen," he insisted. The French student leader Daniel Cohn-Bendit (aka 'Danny the Red') was keen to visit – but the sit-in leaders urged him to stay away to avoid confusion about their aims.

The sculptor Henry Moore was among those to offer financial support. Student deputations traipsed round West End galleries soliciting donations, and travelled in a battered Land Rover to art schools across the country spreading the message and encouraging similar protests. Several of the students' immediate grievances were quickly redressed but as the occupiers gathered confidence their demands expanded in scope.

Some of the students kept aloof from the sit-in, worried about the impact on their studies. The greater number, including those with no particular political loyalty, were caught up in the exhilaration of the moment. And those involved reckon that there were perhaps 150 students – there were approaching a thousand altogether – who formed the bedrock of the protest.

An editorial in *The Times* was broadly sympathetic:

> Che Guevarism has contributed an élan and some theoretical clothing for English students in protest, but what has principally moved them is specific discontent about their art and work as students. ... That is why the hubbub has lasted longer and been carried farther at art colleges than elsewhere. ...
>
> The Hornsey students, the prime movers of the revolt, have set out clearly the changes they are seeking ... they want things to be more fluid, less academic and less examined. The informal and wayward character of artistic talent lends colour to these ideas. But the students also want their courses to be more relevant to the world in which they will be working.

If only the college authorities had been similarly enlightened!

One of the grimmest moments came when the authorities turned to a private security firm which – in the early hours of 4th July – brought along guard dogs in a half-hearted attempt to prise out the occupiers. The handful of students inside the building that night quickly summoned reinforcements who scaled the back fence and clambered across the college roof to strengthen numbers.

One of the guards, sporting a Hitler-style moustache, told a TV news team that stopping students 'trespassing' on the college site was an 'impossible task' and that the dogs would only be deployed if the students got 'out of hand'. He cheerfully admitted that the occupying students were "very peaceful – they are a very good crowd, actually." Footage showed students stroking and patting the alsatians – which were also, apparently, fed doughnuts from the sit-in canteen. A compromise was reached: the security firm would be seen on TV nailing the college windows shut ... but the back gate would be left open.

But the sit-in could not keep going indefinitely. A truce of sorts was arranged and the principal and staff returned in mid-July – but the college was then promptly closed until November. The principal showed a vindictiveness towards the perceived student ringleaders and their sympathisers among the teaching staff which still rankles among those who lived through the affair.

Nick Wright, the student union president, was served with an injunction. "All my degree work had been stored in a Students' Union office. I found it in a bin and it had been burnt, including a film I had made. So I had no portfolio work and they wouldn't let me back in the college."

For many of those most involved in the sit-in, it had been a tumultuous few weeks. "Art students have a sense of humour and a sense of the absurd," says David Poston. "It was dreadfully stressful but at times enormously funny – and there was a great sense of camaraderie." There had to be for, as Kim Howells recalls, the mood would "swing with rapidity from blissful euphoria to mad paranoia and back again."

At the end of it all, quite a few students had breakdowns. "It all went totally toxic," according to Jane Perryman. "Lots of people didn't get their degree. Lots of teachers were sacked. It all went wrong really as the authorities took the power back."

A feature of almost all the student protests of that summer was that those in authority at the start of the revolt were still in control when it ended. But 1968 gave voice to a generation – it remains a beacon of political creativity and protest. Hornsey, more than most, achieved some successes. The sit-in stimulated a debate about art education which led eventually to far-reaching change, if not quite the sort of reforms the students had advocated. Hornsey College of Art became part of Middlesex

don't let the bastards grind you down

ISSUED BY AMHCA

Polytechnic (now Middlesex University) five years after the occupation –
and the Crouch End Hill site remained in use into the 1980s.

All the Hornsey students of '68 vintage that we've spoken to share a sense
of pride in being part of the sit-in. Art students have a knack for getting their
ideas noticed. Memorable posters emerged out of the protest – Martin
Walker came up with his landmark 'Don't Let the Bastards Grind You Down'
when a group of school students visited the sit-in and wanted to know how
to do a lino-cut; the story was told in film; the Institute of Contemporary
Arts staged an exhibition; happenings were organised, including – the
following year – a weep-in and mock funeral to mark 'the death of Hornsey
Hope'. And students and sympathetic staff collaborated in a Penguin
paperback, *The Hornsey Affair*, in which they were given full rein to set out
their view of what happened and what they were trying to achieve.

"For six weeks they reasserted in practice the age-old ideal of the
university as a community of learning," the back cover declared. "That
this assertion had to be achieved by a revolutionary act is a bitter
comment on our current attitudes towards education; that it was crushed
in the way it was is tragic."

6 | The *Express* 'Sleep-In'

The protesting Hornsey students got a lot of attention in the popular press – not a lot of it positive. One news photo in particular was widely circulated – indeed it's still making money for Getty Images – and just as widely resented by many of the students. It showed eight conspicuously well-dressed and good-looking women students peering through the closed gates of the college.

The *Daily Express* published the photo prominently with the wink-wink headline: 'Gates close as students start big sleep-in'. That same issue had as its front-page splash: 'RED DANNY DEFIES DE GAULLE' about Daniel Cohn-Bendit and the student uprising in Paris. Everywhere, students were making the political weather.

The *Express* was certainly quick off the mark on the Hornsey story. The photo and report appeared in print before the students had woken up – perhaps even before they had gone to sleep – on the first night of the sit-in. It seems that a *Hornsey Journal* reporter may have been moonlighting for a Fleet Street paper or at least had tipped them off.

Chrissie Charlton, now a graphic designer with her own company specialising in typography and letterpress printing, was then a nineteen-year old fresh from Newcastle on her foundation year at Hornsey. She's the woman on the far right of the photo.

"They hand-picked some nice-looking dolly birds," she recalls, a touch resentfully. "I was sitting around in the main hall and a chap came over and asked: 'Would you be interested in a photo?' We were young. We didn't realise until we got to the gates that we were all women." The banner was already in place, but she believes that the gates were closed to make the photo more effective.

Charlton was political and supported the causes of the day: Ban the Bomb, anti-Vietnam, and – buttressed by her love of soul music – America's civil rights movement. She remembers that Julie Driscoll's psychedelia-tinged 'This Wheel's On Fire' was one of the songs of the moment. "We were very wrapped up in the spirit of the time."

When Charlton saw the photo in the *Express*, she was uneasy. "I felt 'oh dear', because I could see the manipulation. I was thrilled to be there, thrilled to be in the photo and under that banner, but not at all thrilled to be in a row of rather vacuous, nice-looking girls."

The students wanted their protest to be noticed, and went to some trouble to ensure that it was. Nick Wright says that as far as he remembers, there wasn't much criticism of the image at the time. "The women in the photo were mainly fashion students. Press photographers take pictures of attractive, well-dressed women all the time."

Other veterans of the sit-in have a different recollection. "Everyone was really angry about it," Jane Perryman recalls, "but that might have been the beginning or our awareness of how the media worked." Her then husband, Kim Howells, also remembers being "very cheesed off –

it was designed to trivialise what was going on at the college. We were very careful after that to warn everybody about the sniffers sent up to Hornsey from Fleet Street."

Some reporters were certainly on the look-out for stories which might titillate and outrage their readers. Students recall that a couple were uncovered by a press hack sharing a sleeping bag – but the story wasn't as good as it seemed: the couple were married (and to each other).

Women veterans of the Hornsey occupation have varying memories of how gender shaped their student days and the sit-in. "It's something that never occurred to me," one commented. "We all drank together, we all went on holiday together, we went to the cinema together. If you bought your round, you were totally one of the group."

Jane Perryman, who was later active in the Women's Liberation movement of the Seventies, looks back with pride on the protest, but with a shudder about the sexism that ran through it. Women, she recalls, cooked and served at the sit-in canteen and kept the college switchboard going – but of the 'stars' among the students, the activists who held forth most frequently at the open meetings, just one was a woman.

'Making the Tea; Fucking on Demand' – that's what Jane Perryman says first comes to mind when she reflects on the occupation. She's now a ceramic artist and the phrase resonates so strongly with her, she recently made a ceramic plaque bearing those words. "Heartfelt," she declares, "but not in a heavy way."

During the protest, the students set up a press desk both to help reporters and to keep an eye on what they were up to, and they also kept a cuttings book of news coverage. The *Express* photo, according to another Hornsey student activist, David Poston, showed how the tabloids were "hell bent on sexist trivialisation" – but he sees it also as "an encouraging reminder of how rapidly we learned and became less biddable."

On the other hand, even tacky news coverage got word around about the sit-in. "We were gullible and we wanted publicity," Chrissie Charlton muses, "... and that photograph did get us publicity."

7 | Transported to Truro

In a locality so replete with public art, the mosaic at the Railway Tavern can easily get overlooked. But it has a charm that deserves attention. Take a look for yourself!

The tavern, at the foot of Crouch End Hill, is a stand-out piece of mid-1930s mock Tudor – a style at that time so popular with builders of suburban pubs that it became known as 'brewers' Tudor'. The inn's choice of name is a touch perplexing. Crouch End Station, at the top of the hill, was then an active commuter stop, but the nearest mainline station, heading north out of King's Cross and St Pancras, is the best part of a mile away. It's

a bit like calling a pub half-way along a straight stretch of road The Junction (OK, there's a pub in Kentish Town that matches that description – we'll let it rest).

And the mosaic on the north-facing flank wall – it's lovely, but is it N8? It shows a fox looking over an urban nightscape dominated by a steam train crossing an imposingly grand viaduct. The same design features on the signboard.

The artist is Tessa Hunkin, and this is a personal favourite among her many mosaics. She composed a similar signboard-style mosaic for what was – and still is – her local, The Enterprise on Red Lion Street in

Holborn. "It was a daunting challenge because I knew I would have to look at it every day," she says, but the story of the missions of HMS Enterprise in the 1840s and '50s to search for Sir John Franklin's missing Arctic expedition provided plenty of inspiration. The design shows a polar bear on a small iceberg looking out on a fully-rigged sailing ship.

That mosaic sign led to a similar commission for The Railway. "I wanted it to be a companion piece so needed to have an animal," Tessa Hunkin recalls. "As a Londoner I always associate foxes with railways as the tracks are their pathways through the city."

"As for the rest of the design, the hilly setting of Crouch End brought back an image from my own romanticised memory of Truro in Cornwall. It is a town in a steep valley with a fine viaduct rising above it. My father was brought up there because his father, my grandfather, was the Bishop of Truro, and he always talked of it fondly with a far-away look in his eyes. The steam trains were part of his memories and I think they fused together in my mind as a romantic image of far away and long ago. And I hoped people might like to be transported there, if only in their mind's eye."

Of course by the time Tessa transplanted Truro to Crouch End Hill, the local station had been closed to passenger traffic for more than half-a-century. "I suppose that excuses me," she says, "for picturing an entirely imaginary railway."

8 | A Simple Twist of Fate

The defining aspect of an urban myth is not that it's true – manifestly, if it's slam-dunk cold fact it's not a myth – nor that it could be true, but that it should be true. It's the sort of story that sounds barely credible but could just have happened – and that you want to believe did happen.

Well, for quarter-of-a-century Crouch End has been home to one of London's most enduring and delightful urban myths, retold in pubs and newspapers, fanzines and chat rooms and even in a TV comedy. It feels almost like heresy to subject this tale to scrutiny. So, if you are a true believer, the sort of person who puts faith above fact, then just skip the rest of this chapter.

OK, so let's start with what we know to be true. Dave Stewart who, with Annie Lennox, formed the band Eurythmics, at one time lived locally. He had a recording studio based in part of the former Congregational Church and church hall at the foot of Crouch Hill – at 145 Crouch Hill, to be precise. 'Sweet Dreams' was recorded here – and Adele, U2, Radiohead and Mumford & Sons are among those with a connection to the place.

Anyway, Dave Stewart knew Bob Dylan, who came to the studio and was seen out and about around in Crouch End and patronised a couple of the local restaurants (Banners on Park Road still has a plaque reading 'Bob Dylan sat at this table August 1993'). Bob was even shown round a house in the area which was for sale, an 'Edwardian semi' on Birchington Road, apparently.

But the urban myth is about the very first time Dylan headed to N8 to call on Dave. Here's the story as told by Russell Clarke, the self-styled Rock'n'Roll Routemaster, in a letter to *The Times* – yep, *THE Times*, not the *Fortean Times*, the *Crouch End Times* or any other, lesser title – in 2012:

> In 1985 Stewart had been working in Los Angeles with Bob Dylan and invited him to stop by his recording studio any time he was in London. Some months later Dylan decided to visit him and asked a taxi driver to take him to the address in Crouch End – there's a Crouch Hill, a Crouch End Hill, a Crouch Hall to name but three. Dylan knocked at the front door of a house where he had been dropped off and asked the lady who answered if Dave was in. The woman said he was out but would be back in twenty minutes and invited Dylan to come in and wait.
>
> Twenty minutes later, Dave – a plumber rather than a rock star – returned and asked if there were any messages, to which his wife said: "No, but Bob Dylan's in the living room having a cup of tea."

We told you it was a good one!

This is not by any stretch the first recitation of the myth – the earliest we've found appeared in print in August 1993, and dated Dylan's first acquaintance with Crouch End to the previous year.

Russell Clarke continues to insist that the story is absolutely true – why, he tells us as if to demonstrate the rock solid veracity of the yarn, on the Robert Elms show on Radio London a woman who worked on the publicity side of Dylan's record label

came on air to say it really had happened. Hmm. Others swear that they heard the yarn direct from an unimpeachable source, Dave Stewart himself. We'd be much more impressed if they had heard it from Dylan... or from Dave the Plumber... or Dave's wife... or anyone who was actually there.

The most commonly cited version of the Ballad of Dave the Plumber is that Bob, intending to go to the studio on Crouch Hill, alighted at 145 Crouch End Hill. The problem with that is – you've guessed it! – there is no 145 Crouch End Hill; the odd numbers peter out at 85.

But wait... perhaps Bob was dropped off at 145 Crouch Hall Road? No – there's nothing beyond 73 on the 'odd' side of the road.

All this didn't put off Sky Arts, who in 2017 broadcast a half-hour comedy based on the encounter – *Knocking on Dave's Door* (yes, the potential for wordplays on Dylan songs is limitless) – as the first in their Urban Myths series. It's a fun programme – you can find it online. They set it in August 1993, and cleverly included a scene of 'Bob' outside Banners restaurant. And they just used another '145' as Dave and Angie's place (perhaps they wanted to call Dave's partner Annie – as in Lennox – but thought that would just be too cruddy).

So you can believe the tale and 'Blame it on a simple twist of fate' or take to heart Dylan's protestation that 'No, no, no, it ain't me babe' or perhaps 'The answer, my friend, is blowin' in the wind'.

But for those who like a good, feel-good, story, then 'It don't matter, anyhow'.

9 | The Cathedral

Yes, a Cathedral in Crouch End. Mount Zion Cathedral. A church of the Eternal Sacred Order of Cherubim and Seraphim. It's splendid – large, light, bright and wonderfully well-kept. And its services are in Yoruba – a language widely spoken in south-west Nigeria and in neighbouring Benin – as well as in English.

This is Park Chapel, the old Congregational church in the heart of Crouch End – built in the mid-1850s and repeatedly extended. It sports a spacious gallery and was designed to provide seating for almost 1,500 worshippers. An adjoining hall was added in the 1890s – from the street they look to be the same building – which is where Church Studios now operates.

In 1983, a Nigerian congregation bought the church part of the buildings from the animators Bura and Hardwick, of whom we will hear more in a later chapter. It was in a poor state – an 'empty thing' in the vivid description of Janet Awojobi, now Mother Seraphim and prophetess at Mount Zion. The floor was in disrepair, she recalls, there was no glass in the windows and mounds of rubbish were strewn around.

The cost of buying the building was dwarfed by the expense of making it usable. A Heritage Lottery Fund award helped with structural repairs to the roof and with cleaning the stonework. The church is now gleaming, with imposing wooden beams across the high ceiling giving a striped aspect to the interior. There's new stained glass and devotional art alongside a couple of plaques surviving from the church's earlier incarnation.

The Eternal Sacred Order of Cherubim and Seraphim was founded in Nigeria in 1925 by Moses Orimolade Tunolase, whose portrait is on display at Crouch End's Mount Zion. It's one of the Aladura churches based in West Africa, which have an emphasis on prophecy. The church's founder prophesied that after forty years it would expand abroad. And that's what happened – with the establishment of the first congregation in London.

Janet Awojobi, now in her mid-eighties, was born and married in Nigeria, and came to London in 1961. She worked as a clothes machinist; her late husband, Peter, had a job at the Post Office. Their main concern was to build the church which was so central to their lives and faith – and the portraits of both, painted by their daughter Funmilayo, are prominent in the church gallery. Mother Janet, a wise and kindly figure, is now the much-respected matriarch of her congregation.

Regular services are held in an ante-room of the church with space for a congregation of sixty or so. The church itself is reserved for special occasions, above all for the anniversary service in early October – in 2022, the congregation will be celebrating its fiftieth anniversary, which will add zest to the occasion .

The ESOCS is sometimes known as the 'white garments' church from the flowing white robes – and for the women, flouncy white caps too – that the choir and congregation wear. But that's not obligatory dress. Everyone's welcome. So consider yourself invited!

10 | 'Reclining Female Figure'

It was the last blast of Hornsey municipalism – but what a trumpet call! Hornsey Library was opened by Princess Alexandra in March 1965, just days before the Municipal Borough of Hornsey sank beneath the waves, a victim of local government reorganisation. From 1st April 1965 – what a date to choose! – Hornsey was combined with Wood Green and Tottenham to form the London Borough of Haringey.

The library building is wonderful – light-filled and spacious, and still in use for the purpose for which it was designed. It was built on a bombsite and replaced a much older and more cramped local library. And remarkably for a contemporary municipal construction, it's Grade II listed – in recognition of a design 'conceived on a grand scale' showing 'wit and vivacity' which imparts 'a sense of energy and modernity'.

The elegance and ambition of the design is best appreciated from within – notably on the staircase leading to the gallery and upper floor. There can be found a spectacular engraved window – designed by Frank Mitchell, a senior lecturer at Hornsey College of Art – telling the story of the borough from 1500, the approximate date of the Hornsey church tower, right up until the construction of the library itself.

This was a borough staking a claim on the good opinion of future generations.

That's probably why the borough's coffers were drained a little bit more than strictly necessary, to fund a small pool and fountain against the library's west-facing wall. And amid the water is an eye-catching bronze sculpture by T.B. Huxley-Jones. The work is sometimes simply described as 'a reclining female figure'. It needs a name – any suggestions?

The local press tried to drum up a story about the statue even before it was in place. "Will there be an outrage?" one newspaper asked, almost inviting 'Furious, Ferme Park Road' to put pen to paper, as it reported that the ornamental fountain would "feature a nude figure of a woman." It doesn't – whether Huxley-Jones conducted a modest cover-up to avoid Crouch End's censure or never intended to go all the way, we just don't know.

The statue is a graceful representation of a thin, elongated woman pivoted on a small column. Her legs are extended and feet splayed as if she's dipping her toes in the water, and her hands are raised at each side of her chest perhaps to maintain her balance or as protection from the fountain spray.

The figure is viewed fondly and indulgently by locals but doesn't get a lot of attention. It is a little tucked away; the water in the pool is often dank and unappetising; the fountains don't often function; and the female figure looks out onto another municipal survival, Crouch End's public toilets – it's great that the loos are still open but they don't exactly add allure to the spot.

Huxley-Jones was also responsible for the statue of the Greek god Helios and the fountain at the heart of what was BBC Television Centre in White City, and the marvellous Joy of Life fountain at Hyde Park. His fountain sculptures tend to be, well, sort of stretched – 'attenuated' is the word architectural historians use – but they do have exuberance and charm.

And just in case a passer-by hasn't appreciated that this is all Hornsey Borough's legacy, on the library exterior wall either side of the fountain are two brass plaques: one depicts the ancient church tower and the other is in the shape of the borough, includes its coat of arms and Latin motto and reads: 'The Borough of Hornsey, 1903-1965'.

Lest we forget!

11 | Stork in the Porch

Crouch End has always seen itself as a cut above much of North London – spacious, salubrious... 'Healthy Hornsey', to quote the title

of a guide to the borough from more than a century ago. But as the area was developed, many of the grander houses and their grounds were swallowed up by newly-built terr- aced housing.

Most of these weren't the cramped, anonymous rows of houses built for those forced out of central London by slum clearances and road building. The terraces around Crouch End, or most of them, were altogether grander. Take a stroll along Weston Park and the streets adjoining and you will see what we mean. Their porches in particular were marks of social status, often sporting stained glass, ornate plasterwork, and tiling so vibrant it takes your breath away.

It was precisely to distinguish up-market terraces from mean streets that builders lavished such attention on architectural detail – and on making porches into little palaces. Simply having a porch was, of course, one-up on houses where the front door opened directly on to the yard or the street.

Quite the most superb porch, in our opinion, is on Hatherley Gardens, close to the Town Hall, gracing an Edwardian end-of-terrace house. Like so many of these porches, it is at first glance a little sombre, but a closer look reveals exceptional ceramic tiles in red, green, brown, pink, ochre and half-a-dozen other vivid hues, and stained glass including a depiction of a bird – perhaps a stork or ibis or exotic species of heron – which has certainly never been indigenous to N8.

The owners recall that when they were home-buying it was the finer points of the porch design – and particularly the idiosyncratic design of the numeral above the door – which sealed the deal. So you can imagine their desolation when, a few years ago, they returned home from the cinema to discover police tape all around the front door and one of the beautiful glass panels staved in. A burglary? No – but the police believed, erroneously, that there was an intruder and it was a police officer who smashed the glass. "The police were very apologetic," the residents recall, "but we were heartbroken!"

The story has a happy ending. A local business which specialises in restoring the finer points of late Victorian and Edwardian vernacular architecture (isn't North London wonderful!) carried out a repair so meticulous that you can't see the join. It's the right-hand panel that was smashed, but there's no way anyone but a specialist can tell.

12 | Saints on the Porch

Back-street churches tend to be a touch humdrum – cramped, anonymous, easily overlooked. That's not true of St Peter-in-Chains, a Catholic church close to the crest of the hog's back. It's in that tangle of streets where Crouch End shades into Stroud Green. "We are kind of hid away from anything," says Father Sean Carroll, reflecting ruefully on his own difficulty finding the place when he first pitched up in the parish more than a decade ago.

If you don't know the area, then this *fin de siècle* church may be new to you. But seek and ye shall find!

The building itself is, in architectural terms, unremarkable. Compact, certainly – though the church reported a year after it opened that its Sunday morning service attracted almost 500 worshippers – but with a typical steeply sloping roof which towers over the three-storeyed houses on either side. Its real distinction is the new porch, completed as recently as 2019, and the glorious picture window with its depictions of modern-day saints and saints-to-be looking out on Womersley Road. The monochrome images contrast wonderfully against the red brick of the original church and add an entirely new dimension to an ageing place of worship. And it offers drama and surprise to this otherwise pedestrian streetscape.

"The porch is a liminal space – where the sacred and secular meet," according to Father Sean. The saints on the window are "looking out to the world and looking in to where we pray and get our strength."

In the 1890s, the task of building this new parish was give to the Canons Regular of the Lateran, better known as the Augustinians. The order follows the rule of the fifth-century St Augustine of Hippo, whose youth was so dissolute – and whose father was so wayward – that his mother, St Monica, is the patron saint of difficult marriages and disappointing children as well as of victims of adultery and abuse. The Augustinians took the lead in the parish for 120 years, relinquishing that role only in 2004.

Augustinian priests initially based themselves in a couple of adjoining houses, numbers 10 and 12 Womersley Road, now just next to St Peter's. No. 12 – still the presbytery – bears the inscription 'Austin Canons' on the glass above the door. And it's here that the parish's first mass was celebrated in November 1894. The church building was completed in 1902. St Peter-in-Chains was a dedication first used by a church in Rome built to house the relic of the chains that bound St Peter, the fisherman, when he was imprisoned in Jerusalem.

The church porch was of much later construction and, as long ago as 2012, discussion started on a replacement. "The delay was due," says the church's website, in a form of words which suggests a showdown of epic – almost Biblical – proportions, "to the difficulty, not to say impossibility, in reconciling the wishes of most parishioners with regards to the style of the new porch with what the Planning Department at Haringey Council would accept."

The porch almost wilfully doesn't fit in to the style of St Peter's but neither does it obscure the front of the church. It's elegant, modern and is intended – much like the window inside the church marking the centenary of the First World War – as an expression of a prayer for peace.

The windows are the stand-out aspect of the porch, with eye-catching life-sized images of six inspiring twentieth-century Catholics. They are designed to work just as well from the outside looking in as from the porch looking out. There are two layers of toughened glass and the images are digitally imprinted – those facing in being different in aspect and detail from those looking out. How's that for clever!

The St Peter's six are (from left to right):

- **Josephine Bakhita**, born in Sudan and enslaved as a child, who became a nun and spent much of her life as a woman religious in Italy where she died in 1947 – she is the patron saint of survivors of human trafficking.
- **Maximilian Kolbe**, a Polish priest who voluntarily changed places with a fellow detainee at Auschwitz who was about to be killed – he was canonised in 1982.
- **Francis Van Thuan**, a Vietnamese Cardinal who spent thirteen years in a re-education camp, nine of them in solitary confinement – he was named as Venerable, a step towards canonisation, in 2017.
- **Archbishop Oscar Romero**, shot dead while celebrating mass during El Salvador's civil war – he was made a saint in 2018.
- **Dorothy Day**, a New Yorker and political radical who co-founded the *Catholic Worker* – she is being investigated by the church for possible canonisation.
- **Mother Teresa**, instantly recognisable, who devoted her life

to the destitute of Calcutta, founded the Missionaries of Charity and won the Nobel Peace Prize – and was canonised in 2016.

Father Sean initiated conversations about the choice of figures, and was particularly keen to include Oscar Romero, a martyr who fought against injustice but, being aware that he was a potential target, bore no malice towards those who sought to kill him. The suggestion of Francis Van Thuan came from Vietnamese members of the congregation.

Someone pointed out that the porch was heading towards an all-male cast list. That prompted the decision to ensure equal numbers of men and women, and Father Sean is particularly pleased that they represent five continents – not least because his church says its members hail from eighty-nine nations.

Dorothy Day is the most controversial of the choices. She supported the movement to organise seasonal farm labourers in California and is seen as bearing witness to the church's work among undocumented migrants. She also had an abortion when a young woman, before her conversion, and some felt that made her an inappropriate choice.

Father Sean is unrepentant. "I'm very happy with our new porch from a faith point of view."

13 | Windy Miller in Womersley Road

The sturdy, anonymous villas of Womersley Road hold a secret – magic was once made here, animations which entranced and delighted, involving craft and innovation of high order. For fifteen years or so, two adjoining houses welded into one were home to one of the most prolific and successful partnerships in animation. Windy Miller, Captain Pugwash and Pugh, Pugh, Barney McGrew – all came to life in Crouch End.

Bob Bura and his long-time collaborator John Hardwick started working together in the 1950s at the BBC's legendary Lime Grove studios in Shepherds Bush. They worked initially with 'live action' puppets.

When that became a little dated, they moved to 3D animation. Disney led the world in flat, 2D animation but the British (along with the Romanians) were the best at 3D, where puppets and models move infinitesimally frame-by-frame to create an action sequence.

In the mid-1960s, Bura and Hardwick took over adjoining Womersley Road properties – indeed between them they owned 35, 37, 39 and 39A. They knocked through a door-sized hole in the wall between 37 and 39 on the ground and first floors to give them the space required for the most ambitious of their animations. They developed something new in the animation world: stop-motion films – Stop Motion became the name of their company – where each frame represents a tiny movement of a puppet or object.

It sounds simple: of course, it isn't. And in perfecting stop-motion animation, Bura and Hardwick were also improvising and innovating.

Cameras had to be adapted so instead of running continuously, the shutters exposed one frame at a time, rather than twenty-four per second. The background would often be animated too using a specially-adapted surface consisting of millions of tiny beads which, a bit like cat's eyes in the road, reflected light back brightly at a very narrow angle. The front projection equipment had to be modified, in order that a single frame of film would not melt if held in the gate for a long time.

"An eight-second sequence could take four to six hours to film," says Peter Phillipson, who started working at the Womersley Road studios while still a teenager and is now a leading lighting designer. "You had to give it absolute concentration. For example: if, during a sequence animating the background, whilst making the dialogue of a story light up, adjusting the tracking of the camera and the movement of the puppets simultaneously, a slight lapse in concentration occurred, due to, say, a phone ringing, then you would have to start again from scratch."

Camberwick Green, featuring Windy Miller and his fellow villagers, went on air in 1966, about the time Bura and Hardwick moved into Womersley Road. That was followed by *Trumpton* (who can forget

firemen Pugh, Pugh, Barney McGrew, Cuthbert, Dibble, Grubb?) and *Chigley*. These are known collectively as the Trumptonshire trilogy, devised and produced by Gordon Murray and written by children's author Alison Prince.

While those are the programme names which lodged with both children and parents, many within the profession believe that Bura and Hardwick's best work was with the director and puppeteer Alan Platt. It's certainly what won them prestigious BAFTA awards. *Words and Pictures*, adapting popular books for early readers, and a series of ballet adaptations for BBC Schools, are regarded as animation masterpieces.

Not that Bura and Hardwick restricted themselves to a young audience – their work stretched from animation for *The Sky at Night* to government information films to visualising Bernard Cribbins' novelty hits. Some of the rooms at Womersley Road – all painted black to avoid reflections – were set up more-or-less permanently for one or other of their regular animations. Others would be perpetually transformed as new projects came on stream.

"During their peak years in the late Seventies and early Eighties, you would sometimes find three or four Bura and Hardwick credits in a single weekly edition of the *Radio Times*," recalls Peter Phillipson. Both Bura and Hardwick lived as well as worked in the houses on Womersley Road – Phillipson remembers their lifestyle as distinctly 'bohemian'. Bob Bura had been part of a vaudeville act as a child, with fire-eating among his accomplishments, and was blessed with a voice like Mario Lanza, which would sometimes boom around the studio while an animation was being worked on.

As 3D animation became more ambitious, with the use of tracking shots requiring very heavy equipment, Womersley Road's joists became something of a liability. The weight of the camera dolly meant that the animators needed to find a really solid, sturdy studio location which wouldn't give.

That's one reason why Bob Bura and John Hardwick moved to what we now know as the Church Studios at the bottom of Crouch Hill. They turned what had been the church hall, with its rock-solid floor, into a big animation studio – eventually letting out other space to Dave Stewart and Annie Lennox (aka The Eurythmics) who later bought the building from the animators. By then Womersley Road had been sold.

CGI technology has in many ways superseded stop-motion filming, but it can't replicate the charm of 3D animation. And for those who want to wallow in nostalgia, the Trumptonshire trilogy was cleaned and digitally restored frame-by-frame a few years back and released on DVD. What are you waiting for!

14 | Maddy Prior and the Miners' Strike

For most of its existence, Hornsey Town Hall has faced an unenviable identity crisis: it lost a borough and has been looking desperately for a new purpose.

The Town Hall is widely acclaimed as a modernist masterpiece. It was designed by a New Zealander still in his twenties, Reginald Uren, who won an architectural competition that attracted more than 200 entries. The building took the Royal Institute of British Architects' Bronze Medal in 1935 – the year it opened.

The Town Hall is a striking L-shaped building with a curious and conspicuous tower – a nod perhaps to the grand clock towers on the northern town halls of the previous century. The windows are elegantly elongated, and Arthur Ayres – whose work distinguishes the nearby gas showrooms – was brought in to provide a splash of carved stone on an otherwise deliberately plain façade. He worked in Hornsey's Latin motto '*Fortior Quo Pa-*

ratior' – which translates as 'the better prepared the stronger' – alongside a distinctly non-urban motif of hunting dogs chasing boar and deer.

The interior is even more imposing – a grand staircase with spectacular iron balustrades, splendid panelling and parquet floors, and a well-appointed council chamber and mayor's parlour. You can see why it was one of the first 1930s-era buildings to be listed.

The pity is that just thirty years after the Town Hall was built, the Borough of Hornsey was subsumed into Haringey, which alighted on Wood Green's Civic Centre as the hub of its administration. The Town Hall limped on as municipal offices for another few decades, but it has been a sorry decline.

At one point the Mountview Theatre School was hoping to take over the site – that didn't materialise; then a community ownership scheme was canvassed, but didn't have sufficient financial backing. The commercial redevelopment scheme now well under way respects the listed building, develops some of the adjoining space, and will deliver a hotel, 146 apartments, an arts centre, a café... let's see how it pans out.

The original specification for the Town Hall included a large assembly hall – and this became for a while one of North London's leading gig venues, a role which continued even after the mayor and councillors had moved out until, in 1987, the council said it had no more money for the hall's upkeep. One of the Kinks' first outings was here at a Valentine's hop in 1963 when they were still known as the Ray Davies Quartet (or as 'The Ray Davis Quartette' according to the poster). The band came back to the venue, by now called the Kinks – a word which not even the most hamfisted poster designer could mangle – a few months later.

Move forward eight years, and Freddie Mercury had an early public appearance here with a band still called The Queen, a support act for the Pink Fairies (remember them? – their best-known album *What a Bunch of Sweeties* appeared the following year).

One of the most memorable concerts featured a couple of locals – Maddy Prior and Rick Kemp lived for quite a while on Mountview Road, and were key figures in the folk rock band Steeleye Span (biggest hits 'All Around My Hat' and 'Gaudete' – and, lord be praised, they are still going). Steeleye was due to play Hornsey Town Hall on 18th February 1972. But there was a bitter coal miners' strike at that time which in turn brought a rota of power cuts – and the Town Hall was due to be plunged into darkness that evening.

The *Hornsey Journal* spoke of a "great national power cuts emergency," and after reporting a litany of people getting trapped in lifts and falling downstairs when their homes were plunged into darkness during the initial round of power cuts, concluded bravely: "Things Could Have Been Worse."

In that same 'let's just get on with it' spirit, the Steeleye Span gig was brought forward so it would be over by the 9pm switch off. Maddy Prior tells us she had an alarm clock on the stage in front of her primed to go off ten minutes before the power was to go off. It did – taking Maddy by surprise in the middle of a song. Electric folk was all the rage; an alarm bell as an accompaniment rather less so. "I was doing a pointy-toe dance trying to switch it off," she recalls.

In the audience was a young police constable, Chris Foster, a regular on the North London folk scene. It's the only gig at Hornsey Town Hall he ever went to – but Steeleye was not a band to miss. "At 9pm on the dot, all power suddenly went off and the stage was plunged into darkness," Chris recalls. "So they finished the gig with three *a cappella* numbers with the only light coming from the stage hands. Marvellous!"

Afterwards Chris had to walk home in the pitch black to his flat at the bottom of Muswell Hill. A little less marvellous!

15 | AC/DC

Gas and electricity have had an uneasy relationship over the years. As they first sought domestic customers – and remember, before homes came with utilities on tap, householders had to be persuaded of the merits of getting wired up or arranging for gas pipes to be laid – both presented themselves as modern, clean and efficient. It's a face-off that hasn't entirely gone away.

In the late 1930s, shortly after the opening of the Town Hall, these duelling utilities took up position on opposite flanks of the forecourt – a bit like gunslingers at the OK Corral. Their presence confirmed this part of Crouch End as the civic centre of Hornsey borough. This is where the

power lay, politically and otherwise, with a trio of modern – and modernist – buildings which still grace this (of late) slightly flyblown space. Let's see how it emerges out of the Town Hall regeneration.

Rival showrooms reflected competing claims for profile and prestige. They used the same type of brick, the same window design, the same sense of style – they were twins, not identical but not far off. And with the Town Hall, this trinity of imposing structures must have looked spectacular when they were brand new in the late 1930s.

In the power-play, electricity had an advantage of sorts. It was a municipal utility. From the early days of Hornsey's borough status, the local authority took on the role of an electricity supplier. It could almost be described as municipal socialism – but for the absence of socialists from the council. The Municipal Reform label under which Conservatives often contested local elections in London through the first half of the last century was not simply an empty title – they did want municipal authorities to take the lead in providing services and ensuring standards.

The borough's generating station was built on Tottenham Lane in 1903, initially supplying 126 customers. Hornsey aggressively encouraged householders to get wired up to the municipal service, promoting

electricity as 'healthy, convenient, clean'. In the mid-1930s, Hornsey's supply was changed from DC to AC, necessitating six new sub-stations and the laying of eighty-five miles of cable. At about the same time, in one of those signifiers of a new era, the borough's street lighting switched from gas to electricity.

Around the time the Town Hall building was nearing completion, the municipal electricity supply company took over a telephone exchange and other buildings on the north side of the forecourt. The design of their new showrooms was undertaken by the firm in which Reginald Uren, the architect responsible for the Town Hall, was a partner. The most spectacular aspect was a curving display window fronting the Broadway – a statement of Art Deco style.

Arthur J.J. Ayres, the sculptor commissioned to work on the Town Hall, undertook a similar brief for the electricity offices – a remarkable carved brick relief depicting the spirit of electricity, a man apparently naked and almost kneeling, with stars on one side of him and lightning flashes on the other. It's easily missed, high up above a first floor window, and as a brick sculpture with a brick surround it doesn't immediately draw the eye.

Not to be outdone, the privately-owned Hornsey Gas Company –
established in 1857 – set up showrooms on the south side of the forecourt.
They went for different architects, though it fits tolerably well with both
the Town Hall and electricity building while perhaps being the least
architecturally ambitious. It is redeemed, however, by a stand-out feature:
eight wonderful carved stone panels beneath the elongated first-floor
windows, several depicting how gas is produced and consumed. These
Art Deco masterpieces are one of the architectural joys of Crouch End.

The panels are once again the work of Arthur Ayres, who later taught
carving at the Royal Academy Schools and became a leading figure in
the conservation and restoration of architectural sculpture. The assembly
of his works on these buildings, and on the gas showrooms in particular,

is perhaps his greatest legacy. Some depict domestic scenes; one appears to show architects at work designing the building; perhaps the most successful is agricultural in theme (no, we don't quite get the link with gas showrooms either). And as these look out over both the Broadway and the civic forecourt, they are both noticed and appreciated.

In the late 1940s, under the post-war Labour government, both utility companies were nationalised. The gas showrooms survived into the 1980s. The building is now a bank, but the original design features have been respected. The electricity offices survived into the new millennium and have recently been in use as a restaurant.

So the buildings which defined the heart of the old borough of Hornsey survive, indeed they have a new lease of life – though none serves the purpose for which it was intended.

16 | Paul's Last Stand

"It used to be *Mirror*, *Sun*, *Mail* – now the *Guardian* is the biggest seller," Paul Saxton lamented. "That tells you how the Borough has changed!"

Saxton's newspaper kiosk was almost as much of a landmark in Crouch End as the Clock Tower he looked out on. With its closure early in 2021 and precipitate removal by the council, this corner of North London has lost a little bit of its soul

Paul sold newspapers and magazines here for more than forty years – taking over from his father and grandfather, who ran the business for a good few years before him. The cabin that was home for most of his waking hours was about as unflashy as you could get, but it had the reassurance of the familiar. During the great storm of October 1987, he wasn't at all sure that the stall would survive. When he plucked up the courage to come and inspect the possible damage, he was so relieved the stand was unscathed that he kissed the woodwork.

Paul was brought up in Crouch End, though for most of his working life he and his wife lived further out. He had a gruelling schedule – getting up every day at a quarter past three to be at the Broadway on time for the papers to be delivered at twenty past four. When Tal Amiran made an award-winning short documentary about Paul – "It made me a worldwide film star," he declared proudly – it bore the all-too-appropriate title *Seven Days a Week*.

The kiosk enjoyed a great location at the heart of Crouch End – just about as good as you can get considering that there's no tube or commuter station nearby. From his lair, Paul could keep an eager eye on all around. And by our reckoning, he must have sold three million or more newspapers over the years.

Not many of London's old-style newsstands survived for as long as Crouch End's. The one outside Tufnell Park tube station closed a few

years back – so too, more recently, did that at Camden Town. Paul was certainly old school – no confectionery on sale, just papers and magazines, and don't even think of paying by card.

Paul was proud of keeping to his post through the early stages of the pandemic. Takings plummeted, but his regulars remained loyal. So how much did Paul make on a good day? Paul smiled at the impertinence of our question. "Even my wife doesn't ask me that! We're ticking over. Just ticking over!"

The ticking stopped on the last day of February 2021. At the age of 71, 'Paul the Paper', as he styled himself, decided to call it a day. W.H. Smith's marred the occasion by stopping their bulk delivery to the stall a day early. It didn't really matter. By lunchtime, a small crowd of well-wishers had gathered. The mayor came along. Dunn's the bakers had made a wonderful retirement cake, and there was fizz to wash it down with.

Presents, bottles and boxes of chocs were handed over along with the substantial proceeds of a collection. And there was a very special retirement gift – an exquisitely detailed wooden model of Paul's newsstand. The man himself was quite overcome.

"What will happen to the stand now?" we asked. "It'll just stay here." Paul replied, "... until the council take it away." Which they did, with almost unseemly haste.

There was talk of allowing the Crouch End Festival to take over the cabin. Contact was made with Haringey Council – it seemed to be going well. But another council department had already put out a tender for disposing of the stand. Without warning, a couple of weeks after Paul packed up for the last time, the stall which he had kept going for so long was carted up and taken away.

Paul Saxton once said – and not as a throwaway remark – that he would love to be buried in his stall. "It's mine. It's part of me." Happily, he's still going – up in Yorkshire where his wife comes from, and where he's surely the only Gooner in Doncaster.

17 | The Saturday Morning Revolution

However modest the sales Paul Saxton notched up, he did a lot better than the paper-sellers on the other side of the Broadway. But then they only sell one title – and that for an hour or so on occasional Saturday mornings.

Socialist Worker has been street-sold in Crouch End for almost as long as the Labour Party has been betraying the working class. N8 is not the most

obvious of venues, but the heart of Crouch End has a long history of weekend political activity: Labour Party, CND, Greens. It adds to the buzz of the place.

Fergus Nicol and his fellow *Socialist Worker* sellers – they only set up a pitch if there's at least three of them, to ensure they 'make an impact' (and no doubt there's some safety in numbers too) – find Wood Green a busier, livelier location. But they are committed to keeping the flame burning in Crouch End. And they manage to sell, on average, between three and six copies outside the Co-op on a Saturday morning. No, not each – that's the total sales.

Fergus is not your stereotypical revolutionary socialist. He is softly-spoken and gentle in manner; he's a physicist specialising in developing low-energy housing; and he is steeped in this part of London.

He grew up in Highgate in a Communist household and sixty years or so ago joined the Labour Party Young Socialists, who met at the party offices (still there!) on Middle Lane. The branch was influenced by the International Socialists, the Trotskyist group which became the Socialist Workers Party, and that's the political direction in which he travelled. He recalls long post-meeting political conversations at the Queens and lively get-togethers at a folk club at the back of the Maynard Arms.

There was competition, back in the late 1960s, for the far-left readership. Fergus recalls *Socialist Worker*'s predecessor, *Labour Worker*, being sold on the Town Hall side of the Broadway alongside the more up-and-at-'em *Black Dwarf* and an anarchist paper. Three separate sellers all touting their own brand of revolutionary politics – but united by a common purpose… and by the thick skin that anyone requires to street sell a political paper (try it!).

Fergus sold *Socialist Worker* right from its launch in 1968, with the slogan "The tuppenny paper that fights for you". He and others started flogging the paper on the estates off Crouch Hill and, encouraged by the response, made the Broadway pitch a regular part of Party activity. He has been a member of the Socialist Workers Party since its inception in 1976. The SWP's Hornsey branch, hit by dwindling numbers, has been subsumed into the Haringey branch, but the Crouch End sales pitch survived.

At least it did until COVID came along. But Fergus and his comrades are now back in business, we're happy to report. Saturday morning is just not the same in Crouch End without *Socialist Worker*.

18 | Meet at the Clock Tower

The Clock Tower is the glory of Crouch End. There are any number of London localities which have public clock columns – the one in Golders Green is a war memorial – but none which are quite defined by it in the manner of our locality. The tower is more imposing than most, that's for sure – sixty-three feet of it, if you measure to the top of the weathervane.

Architecturally it's best described as, well, heterodox. There's a touch of the Italian Renaissance about the design, which incorporates ragstone, coloured bands of terracotta, red brick and, topping it all, an octagonal cupola of cream-coloured terracotta with corner turrets thrown in for effect. But it has two really important positives: it still tells the right time, and people like it. The often dour Pevsner, in his magisterial guide to the buildings of North London, put his finger on the tower's secret: it's 'jolly'.

It's also a landmark, a signifier of local and municipal pride. The Clock Tower opened in 1895 amid bunting, flags, speeches and other expressions of civic self-esteem. Its centenary was marked by another street party, during which the tower was serenaded by the Crouch End Festival Chorus.

The Clock Tower was built as a reflection of the coming of age of Crouch End – and as a tribute to the man most responsible for ensuring that unchecked development didn't obliterate all the local woodland and open spaces. The distinguished bronze plaque on the tower's south side, showing a bearded man in profile, is a tribute to Henry Reader Williams, who after a career of more than twenty years in Hornsey's service had then recently retired as chairman of the Local Board of Health.

Williams led the campaign to save Highgate Woods, and secured as playing fields and for public use the farmland between the woods and Crouch End. He also, in the era of the area's most rapid growth, insisted on broad, tree-lined streets and well-built houses. Crouch Enders owe him quite a debt!

The tower has served over the years as an omnibus terminus, as a public loo (in the basement)… and was once the main venue for local protest. For decades, when traffic was a little lighter than it is now, the Clock Tower was the local version of Speakers' Corner. And it was the venue for perhaps the most lively outdoor political meeting in Crouch End's history.

Whatever the purposes for which the municipal grandees erected the Clock Tower – raising the equivalent of £160,000 in today's money – you can be sure they won't have envisaged it as a left-wing rallying point. But that's what it became when Mosley's Blackshirts came to town.

In January 1937, Oswald Mosley, leader of the British Union of Fascists, was given permission to stage a rally in Hornsey Town Hall. Just three months earlier, his movement had suffered a major reverse at the Battle of Cable Street, when a mass protest prevented Mosley's supporters marching through a mainly Jewish area of the East End. The meeting at Crouch End was part of Mosley's attempt to bounce back and convince both his own supporters and the public that his style of fascism had a future as a political movement in Britain.

The local left-wing parties were furious that the Borough Council had given Mosley permission to meet in the Town Hall. His ostensible purpose was in support of the BUF Parliamentary candidate in Wood Green – but that was in the neighbouring borough and there was no election imminent. What really rankled was that some months earlier, the council had denied local left-wingers permission to stage a meeting in the Town Hall in support of Spanish Republicans, who were resisting attempts to overthrow the elected government by Franco's Falangists. They were told that the planned rally might lead to "danger to life and property".

"The previous visit of Mosley to Crouch End with his retinue of broken-nosed bruisers is an indication of what may be expected at a Fascist meeting," warned a correspondent to the weekly *Hornsey Journal*. "The attitude of the Council makes it plain that, just as it is prepared to show its sympathy with Franco, Hitler and Mussolini abroad, so it will give a helping hand to Mosley at home."

The writer of that letter was a Crouch End teacher in his early thirties, George J. Jones – 'Jonah' Jones, as he was universally known – about whom we will hear more. At this time, he was secretary of the Hornsey branch of the Communist Party and of the local cross-party Aid Spain Committee.

In spite of similar protests from the local Labour Party, Mosley's meeting went ahead. The *Hornsey Journal* – unused to quite such drama on its patch – deployed four reporters to cover the rally and the demonstration outside and devoted two pages to the story.

'The Leader' wore a black shirt in breach of the Public Order Act, which had been passed hurriedly after Cable Street and banned political uniforms. "From this platform to-night," Mosley declared, "I invite the Government to prosecute me for wearing this shirt if they deem it to be illegal." And just to underline the point, the fascist newspaper *Action* put on its front page, under the headline "MOSLEY'S CHALLENGE", a photo of "Sir Oswald, in his Black Shirt, at the Town Hall, Hornsey."

While most of the protestors were gathered outside the Town Hall, a few managed to get in to the hall – and tempers rose when one heckler challenged the openly anti-semitic Mosley to admit that his first wife, who had died a few years earlier, was of Jewish descent (which, just to confuse matters, she wasn't).

The violence was hardly on the scale of Cable Street, but the venom of Mosley's supporters shocked the *Hornsey Journal*:

SIR OSWALD, IN HIS BLACK SHIRT, AT THE TOWN HALL, HORNSEY

Four men and one woman were ejected [from the Town Hall], and in the cases of the men unnecessary brutality was used by the Fascist stewards in the course of their duty. Mounted police were called to clear the crowds from the courtyard of the Town Hall after the meeting and during the melée a sergeant was unseated when his horse reared and was injured by one of the Fascist cars. Fascist "storm troopers" from their headquarters travelled in a large, black motor-coach, with its squat windows protected by thick mesh wire.

A protest meeting called by the Labour and Communist parties and the National Council for Civil Liberties gathered at the Clock Tower. Dorothy Woodman, a noted socialist journalist, represented Labour while Jonah Jones spoke for the Communists. The meeting was entirely peaceful, which was more than can be said for a parallel gathering of demonstrators a short distance away outside the Town Hall.

This group, composed mostly of young men and women [the *Hornsey Journal* reported], sang the "Internationale" with upraised clenched fists and chanted in unison "Mosley, Mosley, we want Mosley" and there were other cries of "Popular Front". Some who attempted to enter the hall were turned back by a strong body of police who were guarding the entrance.

Jonah Jones was one of those who tried and failed to get into the hall.

Once the rally was over and Mosley and his bandwagon had moved on, the anti-fascist demonstrators re-assembled around the Clock Tower:

Long after Mosley and his thugs had gone away the crowds stayed to hear what the working-class representatives of Hornsey had to say [according to a Communist publication]. … Mounted police went round the Tower moving the people about. Until 11 o'clock that night Jones conducted the rally. Feeling burned high. … A man living five minutes away from the Town Hall could hear the 'Internationale' clearly ringing out from the Clock Tower meeting.

Jonah Jones made his second speech of the evening and led the crowd in giving three cheers for the British volunteers fighting against fascism in Spain.

That evening laid the foundations of Jones's local political reputation. And it confirmed the Clock Tower and adjoining part of the Broadway as a venue for political stump orators, a style of activism which has now all but disappeared, but was for a century or more a key way of winning a following for radical or unorthodox viewpoints.

Jonah Jones was a solid rather than an inspired speaker but he remained a regular at outdoor speaking pitches for the rest of his life – much to the embarrassment of his daughter, Frances. "When I was a teenager, my father was still standing on Crouch End Broadway, preaching to the converted. I was terribly teased at school."

When the *Hornsey Journal* came to write Jones's obituary, almost a quarter of a century after the Mosley protest, it paid particular tribute to his resilience as a soapbox orator. 'There was no more assiduous street-corner speaker... he was a familiar earnest figure on his rostrum at Crouch End Clock-tower.' And it added waspishly: 'He was never discouraged by the fact that he might not have an audience.'

19 | "Jones for Hornsey"

Our locality hardly comes across as the sort of red bastion which would once have been termed a 'Little Moscow', but in the (admittedly very restricted) universe of Communist electoral high points, Hornsey has quite a claim to fame. It delivered the biggest Communist vote in any English constituency in the 1945 general election – the election which was the high-water-mark of CP success.

Post-war Britain swung sharply to the left, and the country returned the most radical and reforming government we've ever had: the first Labour majority government, led by Clement Attlee. Labour won twice as many Commons seats as the Conservatives... and a couple of Communist MPs were elected on Labour's coat-tails.

Here in Hornsey, George 'Jonah' Jones – who had been so prominent, as we have seen, in the anti-Mosley protests and in opposing Spanish fascism – polled more than 10,000 votes as the Communist Party candidate. Impressive! But not enough to win the seat. Indeed, Jonah came third – a little behind Labour and a long way behind the victorious Conservative candidate. A few miles away in Mile End and Stepney, Phil Piratin won as a Communist with a tally barely half of Jonah's – a reflection of the impact of the Blitz and wartime evacuation on that dockside area of the East End.

Hornsey was unlikely territory for the hard left. It was then a rock-solid Conservative seat – the area had never had a Liberal or Labour MP (indeed, it was as recently as 1992 that Labour took the restyled seat of Hornsey and Wood Green for the first time) and there was at the time of the '45 election only one Labour member of the Borough Council. The Communists were choosy about which seats to contest in that election, only standing in twenty-one constituencies nationwide of which just five were in London.

The CP's decision to stand was probably influenced by the vigour of the local organisation – with professionals and intellectuals in the commanding heights of the borough in Muswell Hill and the eastern parts of Highgate; a more industrial, and militant, membership in Hornsey Vale, Stroud Green and Harringay; and in the middle, both geographically and politically, were Hornsey village and Crouch End.

The other impulse behind standing a candidate in 1945 was the profile of George J. Jones – a schoolteacher who lived with his wife and daughter on Weston Park in Crouch End, and was unquestionably handsome (his photo appeared incessantly in Party propaganda) as well as an experienced orator. The Party was sufficiently taken by him to publish a laudatory pamphlet biography *Jones for Hornsey*.

Jonah managed to convince himself that the local Labour Party would endorse him as a united left candidate. "Here in Hornsey we need a platform of the whole of the Left – Labour, Liberal, Co-operative,

Commonwealth, Trades Council and Trade Unions – to ensure the defeat of Tory domination," Jones declared. That simply didn't happen.

But you can see why Hornsey Communists thought that Labour might agree on a single candidate. When Jonah Jones stood for the council seat of South Harringay in the late 1930s, Labour gave him a clear run – though he still lost. Then in 1942, one of the ward councillors there, an independent, resigned. It was wartime and the council had the power to co-opt a replacement. The sole Labour councillor, Harry Hynd, proposed that Jones, as the runner-up in the ward in the last council elections, should be selected. Only one other councillor offered support. The vast majority on the council endorsed the co-option of another independent.

The left felt they were being shut out of local government. Labour and Communists organised a protest meeting at a hall on Green Lanes at which Hynd and Jones shared a platform. On some issues, it was clear that the parties could make common cause.

Jones's only child, Frances, recalls that she was taught to assume that their phone was bugged. That wasn't paranoia, as documents in the National Archive demonstrate. A police file records that Jones was 'well known to Special Branch'. There are notes of a bugged phone conversation between Jones and another leading Communist. And even more remarkable, an informer apparently with access to the CP's London district headquarters photographed a handwritten letter from a leading Hornsey Communist – it's in the archive as if a photographic negative, white writing on a black background – detailing the resources that would be available to support Jones, if the Party allowed him to stand.

Although the circumstances in which the letter was obtained are sinister, the contents reveal the exceptional strength of the local Communist Party. The writer records that there were an impressive 279 members in Hornsey and another 150 'listed supporters' along with six ward groups and two factory groups. The party's newsletter *Hornsey Forward* had a print run of 3,000 and a thousand copies had been sold of *Jones for Hornsey*.

When the election was held, just as the war was drawing to a close, the Communists probably had the best publicity and canvassing operation of any of the three candidates. Labour decided to contest the seat – but their decision to field Bill Fiske, a considerable figure but with no local profile, caused discontent among the membership.

Jonah Jones was the only candidate to live in the Borough, and that was reflected in his election slogan: 'the Hornsey man to beat the Tory'. Communists pulled off quite a publicity coup when they arranged to plaster their posters in the windows of a double-fronted shop – it's now the Fotoplus store – just where Park Road meets the Broadway. They placed an outsize portrait of Jones above the shop door – a photo of the candidate standing in the doorway had just a touch of 'Big Brother' about it.

In the final stages of the campaign, a shock development gave the Communists hope that they could pull off a sensational victory. The president and vice-president of Hornsey Labour Party and five other key local party members publicly disowned their own candidate. Fiske, they declared in a public letter, was "unknown both to Hornsey and to the Labour Party members who adopted him," while Jones "is a Hornsey resident with a fine local record and the strongest local party organization to campaign for him." They urged "full support" for the Communist candidate.

This was a huge blow to the Labour campaign. Jones was able to claim that he had the backing of a large part of the local Labour Party. The Labour leader, Clement Attlee, felt obliged to issue a statement asserting that Labour's candidate in Hornsey was "the only man who can claim the support of the local Labour movement," and complaining that the "Communist Party nominee, Mr Jones, ... is trying to deceive the electors into believing he has the support of prominent members of the Hornsey Labour Party." Labour may well have been concerned that voters might be confused about which candidate had their endorsement – until as late as 1969, the party allegiance of general election candidates did not appear on the ballot paper.

In the end, the Conservative, Captain David Gammans, held the seat with a reduced majority and Labour clung on to second place. But the 10,058 votes Jonah Jones received was the highest ever Communist vote in an English constituency (the CP did a little better in parts of Scotland and Wales) with the sole exception of Battersea North in the early 1920s, where the successful Communist candidate didn't have a Labour opponent.

The Communist campaign in Hornsey had the distinct advantage of local Party premises in the centre of Crouch End – a testament to the size, and perhaps affluence, of the branch. 4a Broadway Parade was the home of the Hornsey Communist Party for a decade or so – a two-storey flat, now above a newsagents, entered from the back of the Broadway. As a child, Michael Prior used to visit the offices – both his parents were active Communists. The spacious office-cum-apartment was accessed up an outside staircase; the lower floor was used as offices and for committee meetings and the like; as he recalls, a party worker and his family lived on the top floor.

Michael says that women made up the core of the local Communist Party in the 1940s and '50s. "My mother had, after my birth [in 1942], organised a series of local initiatives – a blood donors' centre, youth club and nurseries – which had gathered together a remarkable group of women party members who formed the backbone of the local Hornsey Communist Party," he recalls. As if to demonstrate the point, Michael has a photo – probably from 1949 – of local party members, with women predominant, gathering to join a May Day demonstration. He is the youngster standing under the Hornsey CP banner; his mother, Lena Prior, is just behind, with glasses and a light raincoat.

As for Jonah Jones, he was nothing if not persistent, continuing to contest Hornsey in the Communist cause in three subsequent general elections. By his final candidacy in 1959, the Communist vote had shrunk to a little over a thousand and Jonah was pushed into fourth place.

By then, Jones was in poor health. He had a weak heart and had spent time convalescing at a sanatorium outside Moscow. He died in 1960 and at his funeral at Golders Green crematorium, the Communist Party leader, John Gollan, praised Jones for "fighting for the cause he loved until the end."

20 | Behind the Dress Rail

"Can I just rearrange your dresses and take a photo?" It's not your standard request – it's certainly not our standard request. But the proprietor of Change of Heart was wonderfully accommodating. She's very proud of the bulky broken stone concealed behind a rail of 'pre-loved' clothes.

It's the name-stone of Crouch End Schools, dated 1877 and carved with the initials 'HSB', which we assume to be Hornsey School Board. This was Hornsey's first board school. The school buildings next door – which towards the end of their educational life were the lower school of Highgate Wood School – were demolished in the mid-1990s. The name-stone was salvaged during demolition, but had already been smashed into three pieces. It now finds refuge in a corner of the shop – and no, it's not for sale. The proprietor has fended off quite a few offers.

The stone's new home was itself once part of the school. This former woodwork building – really! – was added in 1893. It fronts on to Park Road and is one of the more remarkable architectural specimens in Crouch End. It's the work of Howard Chatfeild Clarke, one of a distinguished dynasty of architects. But how to describe it? Well, part Swiss chalet and part Norman château.

The stand-out feature is a corner turret complete with battlements, which gives a fortified feel to the frontage. This is complemented rather curiously by two much more suburban-style part wooden gables. The ground floor, where the clothes shop now safeguards the school's heritage, was once apparently an arcade, distinguished by matching door and windows with lots of glass and semicircles.

It's all very grand for a school building – and particularly so for a woodwork department, more often based in a shed in a forgotten corner. It suggests that the School Board took a real interest in promoting craft and had some money to spend. Those were the days!

21 | Charles Darwin's Tail?

"Have you seen the monkey?" That's how we were introduced to a remarkable piece of decorative plasterwork adorning a Victorian semi-detached house on Park Road.

The normal fare for such embellishments is leaves, flowers, birds, perhaps a stylised head or two, often bought off-the-shelf from builders' merchants. But here is a monkey, complete with tail, apparently gorging on grapes.

Monkeys are not that unusual in gargoyles and grotesques gracing Victorian churches and public buildings. They are unusual in domestic architecture. But as we examined this moulded capital, it did occur to us that it may not display a monkey at all. Is this perhaps a bald, bearded man sporting a monkey's tail?

And who could have been the target of such calumny? Could it be the scientist who made the argument that men and apes are related?

Charles Darwin's theory of evolution was outlined in *On the Origin of Species*, published in 1859. He followed that up with *The Descent of Man*, which appeared in 1871 and applied his theory to human evolution. This argued that the difference "between man and the higher animals, great as it is, is certainly one of degree and not of kind." He turned to baboons as a reference point offering an indication of how the human race had evolved.

The book sold well, but it was of course a direct attack on Biblical creationism. Those who believed in the literal truth of the Bible could not accept either that man evolved over many millennia or that there is an affinity between man and ape. While Darwin's theory was quickly adopted within the scientific community, his detractors lampooned the proponent of the 'monkey theory' as an ape or monkey. On occasions he was shown with a simian long tail. Fairly knockabout stuff, but that was all part and parcel of nineteenth century caricature.

So is the decorative work on Park Road a less-than-flattering representation of Charles Darwin? If so, it would probably be unique. Cartoons and prints knocking him are one thing; squibs incorporated into the façade of a residential house quite another. But at least let us explore the possibility.

With the help of one of the current owners, we've established that these houses – there are five adjoining pairs of semi-detached houses, all with very similar design but only one featuring a monkey – were built in around 1882. These particular properties were constructed by George Clark, a builder then in his mid-thirties and living nearby at 1 New Road. He was making his way in the world. A note entered in the 1881 census enumerator's book recorded that Clark employed eight men.

In the 1891 census, both houses were occupied by the sort of white collar workers who congregated in and around London's 'northern heights'. In one house, there was a lawyers' clerk and his wife and seven children; next door was a solicitor, his wife and ten – yes, ten! – children.

Interesting, but not very helpful in pointing us towards the evolution of this piece of moulded plasterwork. So we turned to four of the world's leading authorities on Charles Darwin. Is this their man? Well, the first thing to say is all responded, in some cases at length and with an eagerness to help. But do they all agree? No!

First off, is this a monkey or a man gracing the front of these Victorian cottages? "I may be missing something but to me it looks like a monkey," one prof suggested. Another disagreed: "The head is NOT a monkey's! Too human – hairless, ears flat against its head, no muzzle. And a tail, so not an ape."

This of course leaves open the possibility that it was meant to be a monkey but simply not crafted very well. Could it be a take on the 'drunken monkey' notion – that monkeys are sometimes the worse for wear because of the alcohol they consume through eating ripe fruit? Or – a possibility that another academic puts forward – is this a monkey, perhaps depicted stealing grapes, that was then playfully, and in amateur fashion, adapted to make it look like a man?

The burst of lampooning and caricaturing of Darwin followed fairly immediately on the publication of *The*

FUN.—November 16, 1872.

THAT TROUBLES OUR MONKEY AGAIN.

Female Descendant of Marine Ascidian :—"REALLY, MR. DARWIN, SAY WHAT YOU LIKE ABOUT MAN; BUT I WISH WOULD LEAVE MY EMOTIONS ALONE!"

Descent of Man and had tailed off (sorry about the pun!) by the end of the 1870s. But 1882 was the year of Darwin's death, a much publicised event. His funeral service was held in Westminster Abbey. Might this have been – one of our sages ponders – a tribute to the recently departed biologist… but he then goes on to concede this is unlikely.

The two substantial obstacles towards accepting that this is Darwin are that, in popular representation, he was shown with a very big, bushy beard rather than the more modest trim evident on Park Road. And why would someone choose to have a dig at him on display just by their front door? So all-in-all, it is plausible that this is a representation of Charles Darwin, but perhaps unlikely.

And just to add to the 'odds against' side of the argument, an eagle-eyed Crouch Ender has pointed out that there a few smaller, less impressive, simian representations in architectural plasterwork in houses along Middle Lane, opposite the junction with Elmfield Avenue. One Darwin would be possible, if outlandish, but a whole troop of them is pushing things a bit.

But you have to agree – it is curious!

22 | Workers' Cottages

"I've lived in Crouch End for over twenty-five years," Lou says. "I didn't even know Back Lane existed until I downsized and came here a few years ago." Lou now lives in one of the hidden gems of Crouch End. Topsfield Cottages on Back Lane, barely a hundred yards as the crow flies from the Clock Tower and a decade or two older, are a rare survival. This is a row of six tiny workers' cottages, originally two-up and two-down, dating from the initial development of Crouch End as a London suburb. And hardly anyone knows they are there.

The cottages are locally listed and described as "relatively plain but architecturally robust." Fair enough. The charm is that they survive as a row, all of a piece, looking out on a small triangle of grass and shrubs. And they all have a quite distinct architectural feature: tall front doors

which are semi-circular at the top. Not your standard model from B & Q.

Generic street names such as New Road and Back Lane point to this being the initial focal point of urban development here – names that just caught on rather than were decided on. This area began to be laid out from the 1850s. The cottages seem to be a little later – probably from the late 1870s. And in spite of their modest dimensions (about 500 square feet of living space) they were, in their early years, home not just to sizable families but to lodgers too.

In the 1881 census, these six small houses are recorded as home to forty-seven people (including seven described as lodger, boarder or visitor). One of the houses was home to two different households – presumably one upstairs, one downstairs. The livelihoods of the residents of the cottages (laundress, carman, excavator, carpenter, plumber, gardener) all involved manual work. Ten years later, the head count had gone down a touch to thirty-nine, and gardeners in particular predominated. In 1911, a shepherd was among those living in the cottages – a reminder that little over a century ago, parts of Crouch End and Hornsey were still open fields.

Although Crouch End has been mainly white collar, quite a bit of the initial building was for workers who were able to move out of the inner city and commute on omnibus or train. One of the first references to the area in literature gives a rather bleak account of its housing. George Gissing's *The Nether World* was published in 1889. The stygian underworld that Gissing, a Yorkshireman, depicts is not Crouch End but Clerkenwell, a much older and more central locality. But towards the end of this dystopian novel, the key character moves to "the northern limit of the vast network of streets" that constitutes the capital:

> … for the present Crouch End is still able to remind one that it was in the country a very short time ago. The streets have a smell of newness, of dampness; the bricks retain their complexion, the stucco has not rotted more than one expects in a year or two; poverty tries to hide itself with venetian blinds.

You'd be forgiven for imagining that Gissing didn't think much of the place. And there's more:

> Characteristic of the locality is a certain row of one-storey cottages – villas, the advertiser calls them – but of white brick, each with one bay window on the ground floor, a window pretentiously fashioned and desiring to be taken for stone, though obviously made of bad plaster. Before each house is a garden, measuring six feet by three, entered by a little iron gate, which grinds as you push it, and at no time would latch. The front-door also grinds on the sill … As you set foot on the pinched passage, the sound of your tread proves the whole fabric a thing of lath and sand. The ceilings, the walls, confess themselves neither water-tight nor air-tight. Whatever you touch is at once found to be sham.

This is Gissing as the nemesis of the estate agent.

Where in Crouch End could the novelist have had in mind? It's more than likely that such shoddily built housing would have been pulled down within a few decades. But even more likely that Gissing libelled Crouch End, where building standards were distinctly better than in many London districts. Looking at Gissing's diary and letters, there's nothing to suggest that he visited Crouch End. He was much more familiar with Tottenham, where he called frequently on a friend. Perhaps he transposed what he saw of jerry-built houses in other areas to Crouch End, because the name has a certain ring to it and suggests an extremity, a far reach of the city, which at that time it was.

In some way, Topsfield Cottages are more modest than the buildings that so offended George Gissing. They don't have a gate or front yard, nor any white brick or bay window or decorative plasterwork. But in terms of sturdiness and durability, they are clearly a cut above the sort of places the novelist describes – otherwise they wouldn't have lasted almost 150 years.

The cottages were apparently in a bad way when they were refurbished by the council in the 1970s. They are now in much better shape. "I love living here," says Lou, who still regards herself as a 'newbie'. Some of her neighbours have been living in the cottages for thirty years or more. "We usually meet just outside our front door, old school style." How very appropriate.

23 | Motors in a Mews

North 8 Motors is perhaps best described as compact. It must be a candidate for the smallest garage in the country. There's only enough room for a single vehicle, if that. It's something of an Aladdin's cave – a clutter of bits and bobs, tools and oils, all in their place but with seemingly no place for anything else.

The garage has irregular opening hours – indeed it has fallen worryingly quiet of late. The proprietor, Andy – he didn't tell me his surname, simply saying it was a "long, foreign name" – came to London

from Cyprus in 1948 when he was five years old. That's him on the left of the photo. He started working here in Middle Lane Mews – a hidden-away spot right at the heart of Crouch End – more than forty years ago. And he's heard that the building is over a hundred years old.

He's right – the tiny self-standing garage, with what seems to have been loft space above, appears to date from the very end of the nineteenth century, when the development of Crouch End gathered pace. It's a rare, and rather wonderful, survival of an ancillary building – not a house, not a shop, not a workplace, but something else.

So what was it built as? Well, the thing about these really small structures is that they escape the street directories and planning records. So we can't satisfy our curiosity in full measure, but let's recite what we can find out.

Middle Lane Mews was once part of the grounds of Topsfield Hall. This commanding eighteenth-century mansion stretched between what's now the Broadway and Middle Lane and faced south towards Crouch End Hill. Just in front, very close to where the Clock Tower now stands, was a splendid cedar tree. The Hall had seven acres of grounds wedged between the Broadway and Tottenham Lane on one side, and Middle Lane on the other, stretching to a little to the north of what is now Rosebery Gardens.

From the 1850s this was the home and estate of Henry Weston Elder, from whom both Weston Park and Elder Avenue take their name. He was a self-made man – a bristle merchant, making his money out of importing the animal hairs, Russian boar bristles in particular, used in brushes of all sorts. He laid out the grounds of the Hall with some care, with lawns and wooded areas, a fountain and a narrow ornamental lake. A map of the estate shows stables, a conservatory and a vinery close to where the Mews now stands.

By the time the big spurt in the development of Crouch End came in the 1890s, Elder and his wife were both dead. The family cashed in on the construction boom, and the estate was sold. And to judge from the Ordnance Survey maps, not only was Topsfield Hall demolished, but so was every shed, outbuilding and coach house on the estate. Up came the uniform parades of shops with living accommodation above, Topsfield Parade among them, which continue to give Crouch End its character.

In the awkwardly-shaped area in the centre of the estate, the plan was to build a public hall. Plans change. In July 1897, a theatre – initially called Queen's Opera House and with a 1,200 capacity – opened here, the original design having been adapted by the leading theatrical architect of the day, Frank Matcham. He conveniently lived nearby on Haslemere Road in a house now graced by an English Heritage blue plaque.

The venue later became the Hippodrome; about the time of the First World War it was turned into a cinema; and during the Second World War the building was badly damaged in a bombing raid and never fully restored. The main, and rather constricted, frontage was on to the Broadway. The Virgin Active Health Club now marks the spot.

So what has all this to do with North 8 Motors? Well, Middle Lane Mews was the back entrance to the Opera House. What became Andy's garage may well have been built at the same time – it certainly features in a 1912 map. Perhaps this was a coach house or garage available to the proprietor. After all, if you are going to build a palatial theatre, it's good to have your own reserved parking space.

The bigger building to the left of North 8 Motors, graced by a set of wooden steps – possibly also once linked to the Opera House – may well have been the site of Westerns Laundry, the business mentioned in the sign still just about visible at the entrance to the Mews.

An evocative ghost sign and a century-old garage in a mews which many Crouch Enders saunter past without a second glance. It's these quirky survivals which add so much interest to the N8 streetscape.

24 | The 'Outstanding' Queens

There's no two ways about it. The pubs of Crouch End have more architectural merit than the churches. They probably pull in more punters too. And among the drinking dens, one in particular stands out.

Pevsner's peerless architectural gazetteers can be a bit sniffy about the vernacular. But there's nothing snide about its comments on the Queens

– "one of suburban London's outstanding grand pubs of the turn of the century." Indeed, it's the only pub to feature in the photo section of the North London volume. Historic England goes even further: explaining the basis of the building's II* listing, it praises the Queens as "the pinnacle of late-Victorian pub design," and "a remarkable survival, with exceptional joinery and glass."

This spacious street-corner oasis was built from 1898 as the Queen's Hotel – to accompany the long gone Queen's Opera House (later the Crouch End Hippodrome) across the road which opened in 1897, the year of Queen Victoria's Diamond Jubilee. But it's been known simply as the Queens – not its nickname, its formal name – for many decades.

The developer was John Cathles Hill, a Scotsman who was responsible for the construction of hundreds of houses in this part of London – and of a pub with a claim to compete with the Queens, the Salisbury on Green Lanes in Harringay. The suburban building boom at the end of the Victorian era made Hill rich, but his borrowing got out of hand, and in 1912 he was declared bankrupt.

The Queens is Hill's lasting monument: intricate ironwork at all three entrances; sturdy mahogany fittings separating the sizable space into four sections around a central bar; and the real eye-catcher, some of the finest stained glass in any London boozer. Not that this was any old gin palace. The pub props up one end of Crouch End Broadway and dates from just a little after the Clock Tower. It's yet another affirmation that Crouch End was – or aspired to be – a cut above the rest.

The glass work is largely of floral design and in the Art Nouveau style. It was made by Cakebread Robey, a firm then based in Stoke Newington. Its successor company is still in business – as a maker of sanitary ware. Cakebread Robey built a reputation as suppliers of stained and engraved glass to enterprises sacred and profane.

In its early years, the Queens is reputed to have housed the artistes and performers appearing across the road. And it retains something of that bohemian air. In the 1960s, at the time of the Hornsey College of Art sit-in, students regularly gathered here in the evenings. The place was, in the words of one of its habitués, "very disreputable" back then, and would be closed from time to time due to drug raids. It was still a hotel, and some of the college's teaching staff stayed here – which meant they and their friends could drink out-of-hours.

Like so much of what gives Crouch End character, the Queens survived with its original layout and fittings more through benign neglect than active conservation. Over the years, all sorts of modernisation plans have been proposed, but happily not acted upon, and now its listing should ensure that this exceptional pub remains deserving of Pevsner's praise.

25 | Pulp Fiction

The *Hornsey Journal* was for well over a century the local paper of record – reporting on everything that mattered in and around N8. It started in 1879 and survived as a printed weekly until 2012 – the excellent Hornsey Historical Society has an almost complete run. The paper promised that it would have a digital afterlife, though sad to report its website seems of late to have been squatted by a gambling promotion.

Back in the day, there was money in local papers. In the 1930s, the *Journal* moved into its own imposing offices on Tottenham Lane, just next to the Salvation Army citadel which has been so splendidly reborn in recent years as the ArtHouse cinema.

The old *Hornsey Journal* HQ at 161 Tottenham Lane – the scene of an IRA bomb attack back in 1993 – has also been going through some changes. It was a stylish building, sporting bold vertical lines and geometric design. The place has been given a thorough makeover, with an extra floor added, and the Art Deco aspect of the frontage accentuated. The site now consists of six apartments and – away from the road on the site of what was the printing plant – three compact 'mews' houses. The development has, imaginatively, been named the Printworks.

Those printing presses did much more than simply churn out a local weekly. Between the wars, the *Hornsey Journal* was a leading printer and publisher of pulp fiction. Indeed, it almost cornered the market in cheap-and-cheerful horse-racing romances and thrillers ... think Dick Francis, but without the humour, style or half-convincing storyline.

The series of F.P. Racing Novels began in the 1920s, when the *Journal* was based on Crouch Hill. It was on to a winner. The stories were so popular, and profitable, that two were published every month – regularly as clockwork on the 24th – and sold not in bookshops but in newsagents.

Once the *Journal* moved to Tottenham Lane, the presses there were kept at full stretch producing titles such as *Caught at the Post*, *The Nobbler Nobbled*, *Foiled by Dope* and *For the Cup and a Wife*. When we say cheap, they really were bargain basement – retailing at four-and-a-half old

pence each, that's a bit less than 2p. You could buy fifty with a pound note and still get a fistful of change.

In all, well over 300 of these down-market paperbacks appeared; the series only reached the finishing post in the early 1940s. The books are thin – under a hundred pages – and printed on coarse paper. The plots are thin too – stable boys, skulduggery, sleek thoroughbreds, a ne'er-do-well set on sabotage, a touch of romance, and that's about it. Sometimes the storylines were mildly subversive – a love affair between the dashing proletarian stable-hand and the posh daughter of the trainer, that sort of thing. And usually everything worked out well in the end.

Let's offer a flavour of the prose. Here's the concluding salvo of *The Thoroughbred* by W. & L. Townsend:

> Suddenly Jack took his manager by the arm and led him over to where Blue Night stood, her slim head inquisitively regarding them.
>
> There was a sudden tightness about Jack's throat as he pushed Tom Jebson forward.
>
> "There you are, man, she's yours from now on. A thoroughbred for a thoroughbred – and bless you both."
>
> Then his hand stole into Wendy's warm little fingers.

It's Mills & Boon meets the *Racing Post*!

The real delight lies in their cover designs – not fine art, more fun art, with bright colours, vivid images and an ample dollop of mischief and humour. If pulp fiction is collected, it's because the artwork is so engaging. It's a pity that we know next-to-nothing about either artists or authors.

In the half-a-century or so between the rise of mass literacy and the advent of TV as a mass medium, cheap fiction was in huge demand, whether books about sport, detective novels, cheap romances, war exploits or comic-style publications. And you sometimes had the option of borrowing these for a penny or so as members of a commercial small-scale lending library – a service often provided by local newsagents.

It's a bygone era – much like that of the paid-for local paper.

26 | Silas K. Hocking

Does the name Silas K. Hocking mean anything to you? If so, you have either spent too long in those delightfully ramshackle bookshops full to the rafters of novels your great-grandmother might have read… or you've been heading to Crouch End's ArtHouse independent cinema.

The name certainly has a ring to it. Silas is one of those Victorian monikers which is coming back in to vogue – which is more than can be said for Mr Hocking's middle name, Kitto (it was his mother's maiden name). In 1912, he laid one of the foundation stones at the Salvation Army's citadel on Tottenham Lane – a building with a touch of a fortress about it, turrets included, as befits the Sally Army's muscular style of Christianity.

The citadel remained a place of worship into the 1970s. More recently, the building has been the Hustler Snooker Hall, and was apparently being cased out for a lap dancing joint before being reborn in 2014 as a

wonderful small cinema and cultural venue. As part of the building's makeover, the foundation stones – there are four in total – were spruced up. And now Silas Hocking's starring role has once more been brought to notice.

Back in 1912, Hocking was probably the nearest thing Crouch End had to a celebrity. He was one of the best-selling popular novelists of the era – and is reputed to be the first author to sell more than a million books in his own lifetime. Though it's perhaps necessary to point out that he lived to an advanced age (eighty-five), wrote an awful lot of books (ninety-six) – and we're not at all sure who was tallying the sales.

Silas Hocking was born in Cornwall, where his father had a stake in a tin mine. He became a Methodist preacher at eighteen and was ordained a minister at twenty, serving initially in north-west England. His years ministering to those living near Liverpool's docks formed the basis for his greatest success, *Her Benny*, serialised in a Methodist journal in 1879, published as a book the following year, given by the box-load as Sunday School attendance prizes and still (just about) in print.

Her Benny was sub-titled "A story of street life" and was in the genre of 'waif' stories – sad, tragic tales of homeless, hopeless youngsters living on their wits who win through in life because of their fine character, Christian zeal and philanthropic patrons. Hocking was one of the few men who turned to this very dated form of pietistic literature, and even then had to face the scorn of the more strait-laced among his congregation who regarded novels as just as much the work of the devil as theatre and other vulgar entertainments. The novel had a certain amount of staying power and was turned into a silent movie in 1920 (perhaps the ArtHouse could be persuaded to screen it one day) and born again as a musical in the 1990s.

For a decade or two, Hocking combined serving as a minister of religion with being a prodigiously productive novelist. In 1896, he stood down from the ministry to focus on his writing and moved from

Lancashire to the suburban pleasures of the smarter part of Crouch End. For almost forty years, the Hocking family home was at 10 Avenue Road, one of those grand detached villas in the streets just behind Christ Church, on the Highgate side of Crouch End. In the 1911 census, Silas is listed as living there with his wife, Esther, an adult son and daughter and his niece, as well as a cook and a housemaid.

Hocking embraced a wide range of interlinked political, social and religious issues. Temperance was one of them (common ground with the Salvation Army) – and Christian pacifism another. The Stop the War movement that came to life in 2001 to oppose attacks on Afghanistan and Iraq had parallels with a similar campaign a century earlier to oppose British involvement in the Anglo-Boer War in South Africa. Hocking became the chairman of the Stop the War Committee, which brought together a coalition of Liberals, socialists and radical non-conformists. In February 1900, he condemned the conflict in South Africa as "the most horrible, unnecessary, and wicked war of the nineteenth century."

In the jingoist atmosphere of the time, anti-war campaigners were often denounced as traitorous 'pro-Boers'. Hocking's home was said to have been threatened by a mob, which got confused about which house was their target and mistakenly started smashing up a neighbouring property lived in by a strongly pro-war Crouch Ender. Such was the venomous mood, Hocking gave up plans to stand for Parliament as a Liberal in the 1900 general election – though he contested two subsequent elections in the Liberal interest, both unsuccessfully.

The veteran novelist died in 1935, shortly after his eighty-fifth birthday, and is buried not far away at St Pancras and Islington Cemetery. His vast corpus of literary endeavour is now read, if at all, as period pieces. Perhaps Silas K. Hocking might have mixed feelings about propping up what are now licensed premises, but that stone he laid on Tottenham Lane is about the only thing that keeps his name alive.

27 | Working Man's Café

The Lane Café is a no-messing sort of food joint on Tottenham Lane, straight opposite Hornsey Police Station. If you like a fry-up to start the day, you will love this place. It offers eleven all-day set breakfasts, no less – one of them Turkish, and two veggie – and for not much more than a fiver you can have a huge plateful of nosh, two slices of toast and a cuppa. You can see why an online guide to the area describes this as "the perfect café antidote to central Crouch End."

It also has a place in London's cultural history as 'the Working Man's Café' – the model for one of Ray Davies's most memorable songs.

This corner of London spawned one of the brightest stars of Britpop, the Kinks. The creative hub of the band, Ray and Dave Davies, were brought up in Fortis Green. Ray was a student at Hornsey College of Art in the early '60s and later wrote a song about chatting-up his 'Art School Babe'. In 1971, the Kinks named one of their most critically celebrated albums *Muswell Hillbillies* – though confusingly the cover picture was taken a couple of miles away at the Archway Tavern.

Shortly afterwards, the Kinks decided to invest in their own recording studio, Konk, on that part of Tottenham Lane where Crouch End merges into Hornsey. There was also a Konk record label and – for a while – a Konk club on site. Indie band the Kooks named their chart-topping album *Konk* after the place where it was produced. Other groups to record there include the Bay City Rollers, the Bee Gees and Bombay Bicycle Club.

When Ray Davies released a solo album, *Working Man's Café*, in 2007, the Lane Café – just a two-minute stroll from the Konk studios – was the obvious manifestation of the title. The album's cover photo – depicting Ray Davies in the doorway of a café with the late Victorian buildings on the other side of the road reflecting in its window – was taken there. So too were the promo photos and those used in the booklet accompanying the CD, showing Davies with guitar inside the café or looking moodily out of the window.

It's not quite the Abbey Road zebra crossing, but a trickle – OK, a dribble – of Kinks fans come along to the café to pay a high-calorie tribute to their hero.

Ray Davies is noted for his rather languid, nostalgic urban ballads – 'Waterloo Sunset' is one of his. The title song of *Working Man's Café* is in that tradition – a lament for the way the high street is changing:

> Brought a pair of new designer pants
> Where the fruit and veg man used to stand
> I always used to see him there
> Selling old apples and pears
>
> Chatting up the pretty girls
> With knocked off goods in the van

But the singer is searching for something that reminds him of the urban streetscape of old, before everything was remodelled in America's image: "Looking for the working man's café."

The song also featured – how could it not? – in *The Kinks Choral Collection*, which Ray Davies recorded with the Crouch End Festival Chorus in 2009. The album charted in the Top Thirty. Not bad for a greasy spoon café!

I'm not at all sure how many of the customers of the Lane Café would describe themselves as working men, but the survival of this old-style eating spot is a demonstration that the fried chicken joints on one flank and vegan bistros on the other haven't yet taken all before them.

28 | Lotus Blooms

You couldn't imagine anything more humdrum – it's a tarted up storage shed on Tottenham Lane, now used by a builders' merchant. But this is where one of the great British success stories in Formula One and in motor design and manufacturing was born. It's where Lotus bloomed!

A plaque on the side of the building reads:

Colin Chapman 1928-1982
founded Lotus Engineering Co Ltd
on this site in January 1953

Lotus went on to win seven Formula One World Constructors' Championships in the 1960s and '70s, a period when Britain dominated motor racing, and with the likes of Jim Clark, Graham Hill, Emerson Fittipaldi and Mario Andretti, took six drivers' championships. And Lotus produced a nice line in sports cars too!

Colin Chapman combined the skills of designer, engineer, innovator and entrepreneur – and until 1956, when a crash put paid to his own racing career, he drove the cars he designed.

Colin was born on the other side of London – his parents owned a pub in Richmond. When he was a kid, his father, Stan, bought the Railway Hotel on Tottenham Lane, just next to Hornsey Station. That has more recently been a shisha bar and is now a Mediterranean-style restaurant. The family initially lived on the premises. Colin went to St Mary's Infants' School and on to the Stationers' School nearby on

Mayfield Road (the school closed in 1983 and the buildings were subsequently demolished – Stationers' Park now takes up the site).

During the war, the Railway was a bit too close for comfort to big railway sidings which were a target for German bombers. The family kept the business but moved to Muswell Hill – and it was in sheds, drives and garages around there that Colin and his friends started modifying high-performance cars. The main spot was a lock-up behind the Alexandra Park Road family home of Colin's wife-to-be, Hazel Williams, whom he had met at a Saturday night dance at Hornsey Town Hall.

No one's quite sure how the name Lotus arose. It's been suggested that Colin's affectionate nickname for Hazel was 'lotus blossom', and that's how one of the biggest British motor brands was born.

As the enterprise expanded, Colin arranged with his father to have the use of an outbuilding at the Railway Hotel. This at one time might have been a stable, and the front part was used for storing empty bottles, says Gerard Crombac, one of Chapman's biographers. "Although still very small, it was probably at least three or four times larger than any lock-up garage. There was even a small partitioned office area. The remainder of the 'stable' and the yard at the back was rented by a firm of local builders."

Colin took over this tiny area in 1951, though the official date the business started was a year or two later. The first Lotus sales brochure appeared in 1953 – the address was given as 7 Tottenham Lane and the phone number was MOUntview 8353. It was another few months before Colin, who was working for British Aluminium, devoted himself full-time to Lotus.

In 1957, Lotus expanded to take over the whole of the stables building. The frontage onto the street was done up to provide two cramped storeys, with a drawing office above and, for a while, a showroom on the ground floor. At the end of that year, a report in *Sports Car and Lotus Owner* gave an enthusiast's eye view of what was clearly a bustling if "cramped" business, design and assembly centre. In the showroom window was a prototype of the Lotus Elite, the two-seater coupe that went into production the following year and did so much to establish the Lotus brand.

> In the 'Racing Shops', at the time of a recent visit, were a 1957 Formula Two car just returned from tyre tests at Silverstone, and one of the hard worked Eleven 1100's...
>
> A separate 'garage' houses the engine shops, along one wall of which is found a stock of Coventry Climax engines. On a bench work was proceeding, during our visit, on a five speed gearbox / differential unit....
>
> Opposite the Experimental Shops and backing on the railway is the Production Department...The majority of British customers obtain a set of components from the works and assemble the finished product on their own premises. Vehicles built at Hornsey are thus, on the whole, destined for export.

In spite of the emphasis on building new racing cars, the report added, "Lotus will not neglect the development of the sports cars which have

brought the marque world renown."

When the motor racing photographer John Ross came round in March 1958 to take shots of the new Lotus 15, the sleek design contrasted memorably with the fog-laden surrounds of Tottenham Lane. And the new model was speedy as well. At the car's debut at Goodwood the following month, Graham Hill set a lap record.

By this time, some of the bodywork construction had moved to a workshop in Edmonton. Even so, the Hornsey base proved too small for an enterprise which was starting to take off. In the summer of

1959, Lotus left Tottenham Lane for newly-built premises in Cheshunt. Two years later, Team Lotus won its first Grand Prix – and just two years after that, Lotus took its first Constructors' Championship.

The Hornsey birthplace of Lotus has been locally listed – that doesn't mean much but it has succeeded in dissuading developers from demolishing the former bottle store. So far, at least!

29 | The Tower

It's a spectacular medieval survival among the sprawl of the modern city. The fifteenth-century tower of St Mary's, Hornsey, has long outlived the church of which it was part – indeed it has outlasted a whole succession of St Mary's. It now stands proud and aloof, the oldest building in N8 and the most distinguished.

Rather wonderfully, the tower has been retrieved from dereliction and the depredations of many generations of pigeons. Thanks to a staunch group of volunteers, the vestry room at the base of the tower is once more a chapel. The tower is open several times a year to those who can face the 120 spiral steps. The Garden of Remembrance which rests where the body of the church once stood is well-kept and well-used. The occasional outdoor services there include an annual pet blessing ceremony which has bestowed benediction on snakes, mice, goldfish and budgies as well as the more customary cats and dogs.

There has been a church on this site since the thirteenth century, and a will of 1429 bequeathed money for the building of a bell tower. But the amount put aside for the purpose, 3s 4d (or about 17p), was hardly sufficient and it took several decades to complete construction. The tower still has carvings of angels bearing the heraldic shields of two bishops of London from around 1500, and that's the best indication of its age.

St Mary's, Hornsey, was – like so many old parish churches – rather higgledy-piggledy, and the many drawings and paintings of the old church show a charming building but without a clear overall design. In 1832-33, the church authorities decided to pull down the old building

95

and start again. The greater part of the tower was retained and the upper part was rebuilt, reusing some of the stone from the demolished church. The drawings of the old church reveal that the tower had a turret, and in the 1830s makeover a slightly taller turret was built on top of the heightened tower, giving it a distinctive silhouette.

As Hornsey's population expanded, the church became too small for its purpose. In the 1880s it was taken out of use, though the building wasn't demolished for another forty years. A new church was built a few yards away on what is now the site of St Mary's Primary School – a collection box in aid of the new building is among the items now safeguarded in the tower. This was a grand 'perpendicular gothic' structure able to accommodate well over a thousand worshippers. But plans for a tower at the new St Mary's were shelved, in part for structural reasons – the ground wouldn't bear the weight.

So the old St Mary's served as the bell tower for the new St Mary's. There were six bells – and the bell-ringing platform in the old tower still houses wall-mounted panels celebrating particularly complex and accomplished peals. The sturdy wooden bell frame above is now empty, but it indicates how substantial the bells must have been.

Ann Jones, reminiscing in her eighties, was a teenage bell-ringer at St Mary's. She remembers the thrill of being paid seven shillings (35p) for ringing at a wedding. She was put on the treble, the lightest of the bells, but it could be an alarming experience. The tower was no longer supported by the rest of the building, and a peal of bells could set the place swaying.

"As you sat on the seats round the ringers' chamber, you could feel the movement," Ann recalls. "They had to get a surveyor in and he said: no more ringing!" By the time of her own wedding at St Mary's in 1961 the bells had fallen silent. A few years later they were removed, melted down and recast by the Whitechapel Bell Foundry as a set of eight bells for the war-damaged Hawksmoor church of St George-in-the-East in the East End.

"I was sad to see the bells go," Ann Jones laments. "And even sadder to see the church go." St Mary's fell victim to subsidence. The church was pulled down in 1969. For twelve years, the congregation worshipped in the Parish Hall on Hornsey High Street before combining with St George's in an elegant new church on Cranley Gardens, where St Mary's splendid baptismal font, of much the same vintage as the tower, remains in use.

The tower fell into deep disrepair: the lead from the roof was stolen; the timber beams rotted; the whole building was said to be knee-deep in pigeon poo. Its redemption was largely the work of volunteers, who set up the Friends of Hornsey Church Tower and worked with the local church authorities in securing Heritage Lottery funds. As a result, the tower has been reborn.

The vestry on the ground floor is the stand-out part. It is graced by a large west-facing window and elegant architectural features. It is a breathtaking room and has been consecrated as a chapel of ease; it can also been hired as 'London's smallest and coolest performance space', with a capacity of twenty-five. The conditions of use specify, intriguingly: "It is not available to hire for pop videos for gothic rock bands"!

Access to the tower is through the basement, where an array of objects, gravestones and memorabilia has been assembled. The steps take you past the room where Ann and her fellow campanologists once gathered up to the roof with its crenellated stonework, which is bigger than you might imagine and offers commanding views of Alexandra Palace, the new Spurs stadium, Muswell Hill, Crouch End's hog's back and beyond to the towers of Canary Wharf. It's quite a treat.

The tower must be almost unique in having a book – not a pamphlet but a full volume – devoted to its history, written by the architectural historian Bridget Cherry. She quotes the *Hornsey Journal* from the time, in 1927, when the 1830s-era church was demolished while the ivy-swathed tower was preserved: "for that there is a sentimental feeling which will be its safeguard even in this materialistic age." And that emphatically remains the case.

The Friends have also tidied up St Mary's churchyard and compiled a guide to some of the more interesting and elegiac of the graves, among which one in particular demands our attention...

30 | The Faithful Slave

A 'faithful slave' – it's not the sort of inscription that you expect to come across on a gravestone in an English churchyard. And this is not some relic of the seventeenth century, but an interment from the Victorian era.

The story of Jacob Walker is both deeply unsettling and – on the face of it – perhaps life-affirming too. He is buried in a shady corner of St Mary's churchyard in the same grave as his mistress. This is the inscription:

> Harriet Long
> a native of Virginia
> the widow of Joseph Selden
> Lieutenant Colonel in the army
> of the United States
> and the wife of George Long
> died at Highgate
> on the 18th day of June 1841
> in the 40th year of her age.

There's then a few lines in Latin in the form of a mourning epigram – George Long was a professor of ancient languages at the University of Virginia for four years in the 1820s, which is when he met Harriet. They translate (courtesy of Historic England) as:

> A smiling light shone in the eyes, majesty on the serene brow,
> sweet beauty from the whole face
> spirit equal to beauty, great strength in the heart
> chaste loyalty, duty, and intelligence all together.

And then there's a record of the second interment:

Jacob Walker
a native of Virginia
in America the faithful slave
in England the faithful servant
of
Harriet and George Long
and an honest man
died at Highgate on the 12th of August 1841
in the 40th year of his age.

It's likely that Jacob Walker was an enslaved member of Harriet Long's Virginia household and, on her second marriage, moved with her into the new marital home. When he moved with his master and mistress to England in 1828 – the family lived on Jackson's Lane – his legal status changed from slave to servant. In the 1841 census, he's described as an M.S. (male servant) – though what difference that made to his freedom of action and daily routine, we just don't know.

By the time Jacob Walker walked ashore here, slavery was illegal. A court case in 1772 had ruled that slavery was unsupported by common law in England and Wales. That would have affected several thousand people of colour in England and Wales, most working in domestic service.

Britain 'abolished' the slave trade in 1807 and slavery was ended across the British Empire (except in much of South Asia, where it persisted legally for another decade) in 1833. The British government put £20 million aside – that's an astonishing £2.3 billion in today's money – to compensate not the slaves but the slave-owners. Britain's prosperity, and the wealth of many of its leading families, was based in significant measure on the trade in human beings.

On top of the chilling description of Jacob Walker as a 'faithful slave' is the exceptional interment alongside his owner/mistress – hardly the routine way of burying either an enslaved man or a household servant. One account, which only appeared in print in the 1920s, recorded that "an old black servant [Harriet] had brought with her from Virginia, was found dead on her grave a day or two after her funeral, so the grave was opened that he might be buried with his mistress." A nice yarn, but not true. Harriet died from cancer. Jacob succumbed two months later to 'smallpox after vaccination' – though whether that means he died because of or in spite of the inoculation is unclear.

The common grave suggests a strong bond between Harriet and Jacob, who enjoyed something approaching parity of esteem in death, even if that had eluded Jacob in life. The widower, George Long, was clearly responsible for the funeral arrangements and the words on the gravestone. "The symmetry of the inscription reflects the poignant symmetry of the two lives," Historic England has commented, adding, "… it seems that [George] Long wished to draw attention to this."

George Long's own attitude to slavery can only be surmised. He was brought up in Lancashire where his father was a West India merchant, and so inevitably caught up in one manner or another with slavery. George himself was sympathetic to the pro-slavery southern states (which included Virginia) in the American Civil War of the 1860s. The United States abolished slavery only with the defeat of the Confederate states in 1865. George outlived Harriet by thirty-eight years, marrying twice more, and died in retirement at Chichester.

The gravestone is one of a small number of memorials and monuments linked to slavery and emancipation that were given listed status on the bicentenary of the 1807 Abolition Act. It's a small acknowledgment of an unconscionable wrong.

31 | St Paul's at the Priory

The green spaces in Crouch End tend to be a little hidden away. There's Crouch End Open Space and the adjoining Shepherds Cot, the Stationers' Park on the site of an old school and – perhaps the most popular – the charming and much used Priory Park, with its philosophers' garden picnic spot, paddling pool, playgrounds, cafe and not one but two fountains.

Neither fountain works, unfortunately. Curiously, both are hand-me-downs.

The more modest of the fountains, the Metcalf Fountain, was constructed in 1879 on Crouch End Broadway and moved here sixteen years later – just as the Clock Tower was being constructed, complete with a drinking fountain. It's a little like internal exile – being bumped off the centre of Crouch End to a spot which, while more tranquil, is also off the beaten track.

It's the other fountain which interests us here – the one with the St Paul's connection. Yes, that St Paul's... the Wren one... where Charles and Di got hitched.

In the late 1870s, the City of London Corporation took over responsibility for the churchyard surrounding the cathedral, which was in a bit of a state. Their first big project was to install a grand fountain made from polished Cornish granite in the north-east corner. This was near the spot were, many centuries earlier, a St Paul's cross had stood until it was removed either during or just before the English Civil War.

The new feature had both decorative fountains and drinking basins, for horses in particular. A plan for a statue of St Paul as the centrepiece was deemed to be too expensive.

In 1905, St Paul's got a better offer for this prime spot. Henry Charles Richards, a barrister and Conservative MP, bequeathed money for the erection of a 'St Paul's cross' near the site of the original. He had in mind a medieval-style preaching cross, but the Dean and Corporation colluded to spend the money on the statue of St Paul that they had failed to fund a quarter-of-a-century earlier. It does seem a touch unethical… but let's not throw the first stone.

The Dean's plan was to take the fountain down block-by-block to make way for the column and statue, number each of the eighty-two stones and store the fifty tons of granite in the crypt.

Step forward an enterprising mayor of Hornsey, Ernest Arthur Ebblewhite – a barrister with links to several of the influential City livery companies – who suggested that his up-and-coming area of London could offer a good home to the disused fountain. The offer was accepted on the condition that Hornsey would meet all the costs of moving and reassembling – which seems to have amounted to £1,000 (equivalent to about £120,000 today, so quite a lot for a secondhand fountain).

The dismantling of the edifice in St Paul's churchyard started on the same day that the digging of the foundations commenced in what was then the Middle Lane Pleasure Grounds. Seven weeks later, on 6th November 1909 – didn't they work fast! – the Lord Mayor of London and other dignitaries visited Hornsey to unveil the fountain in its new home. The water supply had been connected and the fountain jets were all in full flow.

It remains a substantial and impressive piece of Victorian public architecture, complete with the coat of arms of the City of London. And for half a century or more – during which the grounds were expanded and, in 1926, renamed Priory Park – the fountain remained in working order.

From some time in the 1960s, the water ceased to flow. For many years, the basins were filled with soil and used as outsize planters. Nowadays the plants and soil have been removed and there's talk of getting the fountain working again. There has been for quite a while.

What the Edwardians achieved in a matter of weeks our generation has not quite managed to pull off in as many years.

32 | Homage to Nettie Honeyball

We're straying just a little out of area for this chapter – but not too far, just along Nightingale Lane on the north side of Hornsey High Street to what was, in 1895, the Crouch End Athletic Ground. It was here that Nettie Honeyball and her colleagues took to the pitch for what was advertised as the very first ladies' football match.

Miss Lynn.   Miss Honeyball.   Miss Williams.   Miss Edwards.   Miss Ide.

Miss Coupland.   Miss Fenn.   Miss Gilbert.   Miss Smith.   Miss Thiere.   Miss Biggs.
THE LADY FOOTBALLERS: NORTH TEAM.
FROM A PHOTOGRAPH BY SYMMONS AND THIELE, CHANCERY LANE, W.C.

Photographs survive of Nettie J. Honeyball – but not much is known about her. Her memorable name was probably a sporting pseudonym, after all how many footballers just happen to have 'net' and 'ball' in their moniker? It could well have been adopted to avoid the late nineteenth-century version of trolling suffered by women who challenged gender boundaries.

Honeyball lived in Crouch End, it seems, and in 1894 she established the British Ladies' Football Club. Towards the end of that year, she told the *Westminster Gazette* that twenty-two women had enrolled, between the ages of fourteen and twenty-eight. "The players belong chiefly to the middle class. There are also four or five married ladies who are regular players," she declared. "We don't want any la-di-da members. We play the game in the proper spirit."

She commented, rather optimistically, that "if we improve as we seem to be doing, we hope to be able to oppose some weak male teams before long."

The prospect of a women's match excited a lot of attention – and controversy. Nettie Honeyball, described as both originator and secretary of the club, was in great demand for interviews, not least because she was so eminently quotable. She had set up the club "with the fixed resolve of proving to the world that women are not the 'ornamental' and 'useless' creatures men have pictured," she told the *Daily Sketch*, adding for good measure: "I look forward to the time when ladies may sit in Parliament."

The club announced that its first public game, between two teams made up from its own ranks, would be at the Crouch End ground in March 1895. The women trained locally in an often waterlogged area at the foot of the slopes leading up to Alexandra Palace. A Spurs centre-half – yes, as in Tottenham Hotspur – helped get them match ready.

As a surviving handbill makes clear, this first competitive contest – of 'North' versus 'South' (of London, that is) – was a big deal. Entrance was a shilling (two shillings for the small covered stand) – a lot more than even well-established teams would then charge at the turnstile. Both the ball and caps were sponsored, and would-be fans were advised of the frequent trains to Hornsey from central London. As for the locals, well, in the words of the *Sketch*, "Crouch End ... rubbed its eyes and pinched its arms."

This match wasn't strictly the first women's game – there had been a few in Scotland in the 1880s. But it was clearly a landmark, and the women made a point of insisting that they were abiding by Association rules, though with a playing time slimmed down to sixty minutes.

The ground (according to Janet Owen of the Hornsey Historical Society) was roughly where Campsbourne Primary School now stands. Some estimates put the crowd at up to 10,000, even though most were standing on flat ground and would have struggled to see the game; the sporting press was also out in force, prompting a "fight for space" in the small box set aside for them.

The women were determined not to appear immodest, but were also part of the 'rational' movement in dress and so wore sporting attire rather than seeking to play in ankle-length skirts. Both teams were kitted out in black knickerbockers and stockings, brown leather boots and substantial shin pads. The North had red blouses and brewers'-style caps fixed with hairpins; the South's colour was blue. Many of the players wore white gloves. From the neck down, there was no flesh to be seen.

The *Manchester Guardian* had a 'lady correspondent' present to chronicle the game, who conceded that most of the crowd were attracted by the "novelty" of the occasion. She reported that the match was "an extremely pretty sight" – though without much evident footballing skill:

> Only two of the girls were able to kick with any freedom, and not many ran well, the habit of wearing long skirts and tight waists showing plainly in the violent elbow action of the majority. They danced round the ball when they reached it as if uncertain what to do with it, much after the manner of a lapdog which has accidentally laid hold of the cat which he has made elaborate show of pursuing.

The crowd became convinced – according to the *Guardian* – that one player who showed particular promise was an impostor. "On the North side there was a tiny player who was readier and more active than any of the rest. The crowd decided that she was a boy, and dubbed her (or him) 'Tommy', but how the case really stood I cannot say." With 'Tommy's' help, the North won 7-1.

Among those unimpressed by the occasion was the outraged *Hornsey Journal*: "It is impossible to condemn it too strongly," a columnist exclaimed. "If… this football match is an outcome of the ambition of the New Woman, it should be sufficient to teach her one of her limitations." The *Standard* added its own barb: "To say football was played would be stating more than the real truth."

Undaunted by such criticism, the two teams embarked on a series of exhibition matches across the country – more than thirty in total –

usually attracting crowds of a few thousand. The women got lots of press attention. For the first time, women's football was widely reported and talked about. But within a couple of months of the match at Crouch End, Nettie Honeyball – the moving force behind the venture – had disappeared from the team sheets and indeed from public view. The new secretary insisted there was no longer any connection with Miss Honeyball.

So who was she? Perhaps she was exactly who she said she was and simply decided football wasn't for her – after all, Nettie was an abbreviation for quite a few girls' names of the era and Honeyball was, if not common, a surname then current; or maybe she was a Dublin-born woman Mary Hutson, as some football historians surmise; or she may have been Jessie Allen (or Smith) who was also, on one occasion, listed as secretary of the club and from the same Crouch End address, 27 Weston Park; or in the view of one historian, she never existed – she was not an individual but a persona used to promote the club and the women's game.

If so, it worked – but only to an extent. Interest quickly subsided, and didn't really revive until, towards the end of the First World War, women munitions workers in north-east England competed in a local cup tournament. The Football Association did what it could to kill off women's football, instituting in 1921 a ban on Football League grounds being used by women – a restriction that remained in place for half-a-century.

And it's only very recently that women's football has again started to attract crowds of the size that thronged the Crouch End Athletic Ground all those years ago.

THE
British Ladies' Football Club.

President—LADY FLORENCE DIXIE.

-THE FIRST LADIES'
FOOTBALL MATCH

(NORTH v. SOUTH)

WILL BE PLAYED ON

Saturday, 23rd March, 1895,

UPON THE

CROUCH END ATHLETIC GROUND,

NIGHTINGALE LANE, HORNSEY.

KICK OFF 4.30.

The Ladies' Match will be preceded by

CROUCH END v. 3rd GRENADIER GUARDS,

KICK OFF 3 O'CLOCK.

Admission (including both Matches) 1s.

Covered Stand, 1s. extra.

Frequent Trains from Moorgate Street, Broad Street, King's Cross, and intermediate stations to Hornsey.

Ladies desirous of joining the above Club should apply to Miss
NETTIE J. HONEYBALL, "Ellesmere," 27, Weston Park, Crouch End, N.

Footballs by COOK.   Caps by A. E. RAISIN, of Stroud Green Road.

W. & W. J. Mizen, Printers, 13, Stroud Green Road, N.

Acknowledgements

I am grateful to the Hornsey Historical Society for allowing me access to their marvellous archives, and in particular their holdings of the *Hornsey Journal*. A longer version of the chapter about the Communist candidate 'Jonah' Jones appeared in the Society's award-winning annual *Bulletin* for 2021. The *Bulletin*'s editor, Sandra Clark, has been generous in reading and advising on a draft of this book. I have also been given encouragement and support by other Society members, notably Janet Owen, the publications officer, and David Winskill, who took me on a stimulating walk round Crouch End and introduced me to the Park Road 'monkey'. Mark Afford, chair of the Crouch End Neighbourhood Forum, helped with general advice and introductions. Many others have taken a great deal of trouble to help with individual chapters and they are acknowledged in the text.

A big shout out to Ross Bradshaw and Five Leaves Publications for sticking with the *Curious* brand – of which this ifsthe fourth iteration – through the pandemic and all the havoc that unleashed. Pippa Hennessy has once again given distinction to the book's design and her copy editing has saved the author from ignominy – thank you! Nancy Edwards has designed the delightful map in this book, as she has in all the *Curious* titles.

And the photographs

The undated photograph of the Crouch End clock tower and that of Crouch End Station, both well over a hundred years old, are published courtesy of the Bishopsgate Institute.

The photograph of Bridget Hitler in her Priory Gardens home is courtesy of Shutterstock.

Sally Fraser (now Chandan Fraser) took the photograph of students during the Hornsey College of Art sit-in and has very kindly given permission for it to be published for the first time in this book – those featured at the window are, from left, Dave Poston, Prue Bramwell-Davis and Jose 'Pepe' Nava.

My thanks to Martin Walker and to David Page for permission to include Martin's poster: 'Don't Let the Bastards Grind You Down'.

The photo of women students at the gates of the college was taken by C. Maher and is courtesy of Getty Images.

The photograph of Bob Bura was taken by his colleague John Hardwick and is published with permission.

The photograph of 'Jonah' Jones during the 1945 election campaign is courtesy of Frances Bowman, and that of the Hornsey Communist contingent on a May Day march is included with the permission of Michael Prior.

The photograph of the Lotus 15 in Tottenham Lane were taken by John Ross and is published by kind permission of his estate who retain the copyright – johnrossmotorracingarchive.co.uk.

The photograph of the North football team including Nettie Honeyball is courtesy of Illustrated London News Ltd / Mary Evans

Also available:

Curious Kentish Town by Martin Plaut and Andrew Whitehead

Curious Camden Town by Martin Plaut and Andrew Whitehead

Curious King's Cross by Andrew Whitehead

www.fiveleaves.co.uk

www.fiveleavesbookshop.co.uk